The Burroughs Corporation

Detroit's Dynamic Dwarf

by

Lee R. Featheringham

A case study and personal chronicle of an innovative American
information systems company

The Burroughs Corporation

ISBN: 978-1-312-62354-1

The Burroughs Corporation

Burroughs World Headquarters

Detroit, Michigan

(circa 1968)

Architectural Drawing by

Smith & Gardner Architects, Southfield, Michigan

The Burroughs Corporation

The Burroughs Corporation

Dedication

To all the men and women of the Burroughs Corporation who played their part in creating and giving life to the remarkable Burroughs story.

And, a special salute to Judy Volk and Jim Hughes, compadres who are no longer with us.

The Burroughs Corporation

The Burroughs Corporation

Table of Contents

The Burroughs Corporation

The Coleman Legacy

The Burroughs Corporation

The Burroughs Corporation

The Burroughs Corporation

The Burroughs Corporation

Table of Illustration & Figures

The Burroughs Corporation

Acknowledgments

My deepest thanks go to the Charles I. Babbage Institute (CBI) of the University of Minnesota Libraries for their careful preservation of and research access to the unique information collections residing there donated by the Unisys Corporation and thereby saving massive valuable information from the business years of the Burroughs Corporation.

A special thanks goes to Ms. Stephanie Horowitz Crowe, assistant archivist, who's special attention and care provided during my research visit there in May, 2009, produced major facts and references I needed for this book as well as her offer of professional interest that supported this budding author's goal to make this chronicle and case study a reality.

And, an appreciative thanks to Mr. Arvid Nelsen, Archivist, CBI, for his critical assistance with photo resources and permissions to produce the book.

Plus, a major spokesperson for all things historical Burroughs is Michael Hancock, whose work on the Internet is out there for all interested parties to learn from and share. Some of his work is cited here as part of the Burroughs history many of us enjoy.

The Burroughs Corporation

The Burroughs Corporation

Introduction

In 1986, the Burroughs name left the world information systems scene due to its merger with Sperry-Rand to create the Unisys Corporation.

But, before 1986, the Burroughs Corporation had long before earned a solid and well- deserved place in the American and International business world.

In a way, Burroughs lives on within Unisys via the merger but the story of the Burroughs Corporation from 1904 to 1986 in Detroit, Michigan, is one of a feisty and worthy competitive survivor in the tough emerging computer industry of the 20th century. Its story stands as a major business model and case study of aggressive performance and competitive survival in that period of time.

The Detroit period of 1904 to 1986 spanned a total of 82 years of the company's Michigan existence. It included the early adding machine producing years in Detroit through two world wars and smack into the emerging new computer age years of the 1950's and 1960's.

Before 1904, the original Burroughs company was located in St. Louis, Missouri, for 18 years. In total, including both the St.

Louis years and Detroit years, Burroughs existed for 100 years on this earth.

How Burroughs survived and flourished in their Michigan home is the main story of this book. What Burroughs did successfully and not so successfully is the record being looked at here. What it did successfully was its lasting strength. But, what it did not do successfully is also an important part of the whole story.

The viewpoint of this story is purposely told utilizing media reporting records, my personal experience with the company, and from events in the customer technical support interface arena where the products and users of the Burroughs products came together to do the daily transactions of business information handling.

For more detailed descriptions of the early Burroughs years before it concentrated on a computing orientation, many fine reference sources exist in print and on the Internet detailing the chronological history of the Burroughs Corporation and its predecessor company names. A Table A of Internet References at the end of this book provides some of those history resources.

Also, there are many specific special and unique technical projects in the company's ancestry worth mentioning. These projects laid the groundwork skills that Burroughs used to its business advantage. Some of that rich special project history and its authors are referred to and included in this book.

The Burroughs Corporation

As a general case study and personal chronicle, this book is intended to be a look at the corporation as an American business system that had a valuable legacy and message to offer beyond machines and software. This book is meant to be a chronicle and case study of both the business and personal sides of the venerable corporation – how all of it made up the whole being of Burroughs and its total impact.

The book's second level title-line comes from the industry's nicknaming of seven competing companies (the Dwarfs) with IBM (Snow White). The dwarfs were: Burroughs, Honeywell, NCR, Control Data, Sperry-Rand, General Electric, and RCA.

A-NOTE

As a side note, the book purposely features the last twenty years of the company's existence (1966 to 1986) for two reasons:

1. **These twenty years (1966-1986) are what I like to call the Burroughs "Great Years". The company soared in these twenty years and helped in a large part to build the worldwide computer industry. These were the years of the evolving computing explosion and the years following the Burroughs decision to build and**

open their new World Headquarters in Detroit, Michigan, and be a major player.

2. **Another reason for this particular time period is it is a period when I worked for the company as an employee in customer technical support positions and then eventually as a customer/user. These experiences allowed me to bring you, the reader, a little closer into the corporation as it flourished over the twenty years. It allowed me to tie actual events and corporate intentions together at given moments in time and give you a window into how the results felt and were executed in real locations in real time.**

I'm sure corporate plans and development schemes didn't always pan out for one reason or another and goals certainly changed due to rapidly appearing new inputs. But, tying Burroughs' daily company real-time situations to places where I was present lets me share a living history, which is always a valued recorder and teacher. So, as a motivating basis for this book, the Burroughs' series of sound business decisions and implementations are the story.

This is not an "Inside the Boardroom" story. This is a "Where the Rubber Meets the Road" tale, to borrow from the automobile field. This is a story of a builder of computers and the people who both serviced and used them.

The Burroughs Corporation

Admittedly, this book has a customer technical support focus because that's where I viewed it but everything a company does or tries to do comes to play in the interface between the customer and the corporation's products and services. That's where the action is. It's in the "Field", as it is called, where the sales and support personnel interface daily with the customers in their environments. So, the view from customer technical support eyes is very representative of how the planning and strategy played out (good or bad).

As a disclaimer, I readily admit no corporation or enterprise is perfect or without some employee personal angst. It's all part of any structure made up of human beings with living personal careers involved. There were the usual water-cooler discussions and reactions both plus and minus in the daily work flow, but this book attempts to tell the story of how the Burroughs Corporation flourished generally as an entity and survived during the wildly exciting time it did exist in the computer industry.

One of the most important parts of the tale of the Burroughs Corporation were the combined efforts of the thousands of people who made up the company and the attitudes and enthusiasms they brought to it. There was an infectious "Can do!" spirit there and a whole lot of energy running hard inside the company to not remain Number 2 in the industry or even think that way.

There were also the legions of users of Burroughs equipment who joined their business lives with Burroughs personnel daily and made it all work for both vendor and user. The word "teamwork" truly applied between vendor and customer and amazing results were produced routinely together.

Also, the Burroughs story was and still is a great story to simply enjoy as a real life tale. There are many, many Burroughs alumni out there today and when they meet, the "war stories" referring to the former days are often bound to come up; some more accurately than others. The joy is in the retelling and rereading of how it all went down.

Life at Burroughs did have its humorous moments as all good efforts by good people do. Some of those I heard of or actually witnessed are in this book as side notes. But, the point of the book and its emphasis is still mainly to look at what the corporation did and why and how the results worked out.

And, so you as a reader can tell when I'm offering a personal anecdote, I preface it with the "**A-NOTE**" heading (for author comment).

"**B-NOTE**" entries are side-bar information of facts about the Burroughs Corporation offered as background.

A-NOTE

The word "Burroughs" is often used as a noun in this book in such situations as: "Burroughs decided, Burroughs knew, and Burroughs implemented". That was the way most of us who worked there referred to the company.

The Burroughs Corporation

It also was also simply easier to use this same word, "Burroughs" without an apostrophe and "s" in possessive usage, as in "Burroughs Plants".

The Burroughs Corporation

The Burroughs Corporation

Burroughs Lifeline

Year	Event
1885	Adding Machine invented and patented by William S. Burroughs
1886	American Arithmometer Company formed, St. Louis, Missouri
1898	W. S. Burroughs dies
1904	Burroughs company move to Detroit, Michigan
1905	Company renamed Burroughs Adding Machine Company
1917	World War I begins
1918	Construction begins on a five-floor building next to the main factory in Detroit
1918	World War I ends
1927	Burroughs Farms recreational facility opened at Brighton, Michigan
1929	The Great Depression, USA
1931	Burroughs introduces the "Burroughs Standard Typewriter"
1941	USA enters World War II
1942	Production of the Norden bombsight begins
1945	World War II ends
1946	John S. Coleman named president – Burroughs
1947	The Burroughs "B" trademark is adopted
1948	Transistor invented at AT&T
1950	The first Sensimatic accounting machine is released
1953	The company name is changed to The Burroughs Corporation

The Burroughs Corporation

Year	Event
1957	ElectroData Corporation of Pasadena California acquired
1958	Ray R. Eppert named president – Burroughs
1960	B5000 System Design Project
1967	Ray W. Macdonald named president – Burroughs
1967	Detroit Riots
1970	Burroughs Detroit World Headquarters opened
1973	Burroughs "700" Series machines
1975	Burroughs "800" Series machines
1977	Paul S. Mirabito succeeds Ray W. Macdonald as head of Burroughs
1979	W. Michael Blumenthal selected to head Burroughs
1980	Burroughs "900" Series machines
1981	New "A" Series machines introduced
1985	New "V" Series machines introduced
1985	100th anniversary of Burroughs as an American company
1985	Merger talks initiated by W. Michael Blumenthal with Sperry Corporation
1986	Burroughs merges with Sperry to become the Unisys Corporation.

Ref: \www.home.ix.netcom.com/~hancockm/history_ timeline.htm

Chapter 1

The Early Legacy Years (1886 – 1946)

St. Louis Beginnings (1886 – 1904)

The beginning of the Burroughs business story is the story of a man with a patentable idea and the subsequent birth of a company founded on his ideas in St. Louis in 1886. The company name then was the American Arithmometer Company. That new company manufactured an adding and listing machine invented and patented by William Seward Burroughs in 1885.[1]

The Idea

   W. S. Burroughs' persistent conception and production of a working, reliable adding machine turned out to be a suitable start to a company eventually dedicated to being a leader in information systems.

   Joseph Boyer, a president of the American Arithmometer Company, said the following about the inventor W.S. Burroughs (as quoted on a website maintained by Michael Hancock):

"There was Burroughs with his great idea, greater than any of us could fully appreciate, and with his meager capital of $300. Long before the first model was actually begun his money was gone. But, as his resources dwindled, his courage grew. I used to leave him at his bench in the evening and find him still there in the morning.

When the first machine proved a failure, Burroughs made another model. Finally, the third model seemed to meet his standards. He could make it perform mathematical wonders, so a lot (batch) of 50 machines was made. However, when untrained operators ran the machines, they got the most amazing results. People began to question Burroughs judgment and doubt his ability.

Everyone but Burroughs was ready to quit. Yet the inventor himself was undaunted, demonstrating his contempt for imperfection by tossing the 50 machines, one by one, out of a second-story window. Then he began work on a new model. Night after night he worked feverishly, 24 hours a day, 34 hours at a stretch. Then at last, the wonderful governor that has made the machine foolproof was invented. Burroughs was jubilant. His machine was perfect. His faith had been justified."[2]

B-Note:

Burroughs Key (1) Produce quality designs offering new features

The company flourished in St. Louis for nineteen years producing products over into the new 20th century.

A significant event in those St. Louis years, typical of Burroughs thinking, was the establishment in 1895 of an overseas company manufacturing in Nottingham, England, under the name Burroughs Adding and Registering Company Limited. There was a first example of building an international enterprise that Burroughs eventually did so well.[3]

The eventual substantial Burroughs Corporation businesses in Europe and the United Kingdom eventually came out of this early idea as well as a far-reaching world-wide presence carrying the Burroughs name.

B-Note:

Burroughs Key (2) Implement international marketing

Then, in 1904, in one of the company's major defining events, the decision was made to move the entire operation to Detroit, Michigan.

The reasoning behind the move is buried in time now and mostly speculative concerning what was evaluated and decided upon but the fact the company marketed to business, banking, and accounting needs is a known part of the story. Burroughs served the business and financial industry.

Why Detroit? That decision was made by people long-gone now but remains defining to the story of Burroughs. Detroit in 1904 was a rapidly growing manufacturing center and that industry must have strongly attracted businesses seeing the possible need for new growth for financial services to all kinds of businesses and start-up office operations.

Detroit was also on the Great Lakes iron ore, coal, lumber, and steel making commerce route which was a major business corridor in the Midwest. In 1904, Detroit was fortunately well-situated for the important beginnings of the new automobile industry popping up.

Detroit (1904-1946)

With what must have been a very determined and well-planned operation, the company did make the move of everything and everybody to Detroit in 1904 by rail and settled on a site between Second and Third Avenues near W. Grand Boulevard. This land was in what became the New Center area of Detroit where the Fisher Building and early General Motors Headquarters building would eventually be built. In 1904, the site was somewhat removed from Detroit's downtown center but could comfortably hold a new factory and business offices with room to spare.

The Burroughs site was reportedly built on a cornfield owned by the Ferry Seed Company.[4]

William S. Burroughs was no longer living. He had died in September 1898[5] but his name went on when the company became the Burroughs Adding Machine Company in 1905.[6]

That early Detroit-based company built the long, low brick building along Second Avenue that remained the main offices of the company until the late Sixties. Behind it to the West was the huge six wing factory structure built around 1918. Other structures were built on the site but these two were the only ones remaining in the Sixties.

Business Environment

The "Early Years" of Burroughs covered business growth from turn of the century production to the arrival of major technological inventions one-after-the other.

This period saw amazing change in America, in civic lighting, communications, vacuum tubes, automotive design, air commercial flight, and war technical advances from two world wars unimagined just a short time earlier.

The Early Legacy Years

New technology was continually surfacing and being incorporated by businesses and Burroughs was active all through the period producing, changing, and adapting.

Burroughs Goals and Focus

The early years in Detroit from 1904 to 1946 were initially the Burroughs adding machine focus years.

Burroughs eventually became heavily invested in producing accounting machines. By the end of the early years its base business was mainly accounting and business machines which continually fed the bottom line. Since Burroughs went on to eventually became a major computer manufacturing company later, it's often ignored or forgotten that those utilitarian office business machines were their core business and were continually produced in one form or other throughout Burroughs history.

But, in these early years, businesses manufacturers were also becoming heavily influenced by the technical developments produced during World War II. Mechanical systems and then vacuum tube computers, radar, electronic displays, optical devices and a variety of other technologies were appearing and Burroughs was already doing highly-skilled machining work at the time. The natural developmental links to electro-mechanical systems were directly in the Burroughs field of focus.

Acquisitions

As noted earlier, acquisitions were always a key part of the Burroughs business plan and they appear through-out the company's history. Burroughs management often bought or acquired technology it needed to keep the momentum high.

One of these important characteristic signatory events for Burroughs occurred in 1909 when a company was acquired to enhance the original company. It was the Pike Adding Machine Company of New Jersey. In 1921, it was the Moon-Hopkins Billing Machine Company of Missouri that was acquired.[7]

There were further instances of acquiring outside assets including the Mitag and Voger and Acme Carbon & Ribbon Company in 1949.[8]

Various studied opinions on the value or worthlessness of acquisitions appear in the literature of business. The opinions point to how the acquisitions are used is a major deciding issue. For the record, Burroughs did use the policy of acquisitions throughout its business history.

B-Note:

Burroughs Key (3) Incorporate specific acquisitions into business plans

Defense Business

Pursuing defense work, like making key acquisitions and building international operations, was present throughout the Burroughs history as an important part of how it survived the first sixty years from 1856 to 1946.

The Burroughs Adding Machine Company was there producing products all through World Wars I and II. It played its part of providing industrial support for those victories. The company earned an Army-Navy "E" for outstanding achievement in 1944.[9] And, even more importantly from a historical perspective, its defense contracts were major contributors to the essential Burroughs Research and Development portfolio.

B-Note:

Burroughs Key (4) Market specifically to defense business

A-Note:

While I was employed by Burroughs I had heard that the company was one of the builders of the Norden bombsights used in the WWII war effort. In researching this book, I later found evidence that Burroughs had indeed participated in that part of war production.

The experience of building specialized products like that went into the Burroughs knowledge base to be called upon for later new needs.

Significantly, defense work projects appear prominently in every era of this book, as noted in succeeding chapters.

The Early Presidents

The major five leaders of the first sixty years of Burroughs until 1946 were: [10]

Thomas Metcalfe	1886
Charles E. Barney	1891
Joseph Boyer	1902
Standish Backus	1920
Alfred J. Doughty	1943

As the first sixty years of the company closed in 1946, the next and final forty years period opened under John S. Coleman as president. The Burroughs Corporation was poised, seasoned, and now ready to compete, compete hard, and makes its mark.

The Early Legacy Years

Chapter 2

The John S. Coleman Era (1946-1956)

The First of the Five Final Leaders

John S. Coleman was a salesman, which was one of the common factors for most of the Burroughs management heads for the last forty years of the company.

Burroughs always maintained a sales focus as a company and he, Coleman, was one of their own, an insider, with sales experience and certainly product knowledge.

He took over the reins of the adding machine company after the end of World War II. Burroughs had been doing business since 1886 at the time and had played its part in support of two war efforts. Now, in 1946, when Mr. Coleman took over, the company faced the post-war future.

To say Mr. Coleman came to power at a momentous moment in the company's history was no exaggeration. World War II had rapidly pushed the arrival and inclusion of the electronic age into the business arena and Mr. Coleman was taking over a company skilled in mechanical precision now coming into a burgeoning electro-mechanical and electronic world.

A positive reading by the media occurred in 1961 when it looked back at his tenure: "In 1946, John S. Coleman named president. He got plants in Detroit, New Jersey, New York, Ohio, California, England, Scotland, France, and Brazil. (He was)…a

11

Burroughs salesman – high caliber. (Goals)…get technical information fast and business systems. (Burroughs) morale high - sparked by Coleman's enthusiastic leadership." [11]

Business Environment

Politically, the country was governed under the presidencies of Harry S. Truman and Dwight D. Eisenhower during the Coleman years at Burroughs. Both of those presidencies were caught up in and felt the pressures of progress and change just as Burroughs and every other aspect of American business did.

In that period, the Korean War dominated the country's foreign policy as well as continuing Cold War issues.

The country had emerged from WWII with major changes in world-wide expectations that life would be better and new manufactured products would surface using new technologies.

From a technology standpoint, what was going on behind the Burroughs usual building and marketing of adding machines and business calculators was nothing short of a technology tidal wave.

The World War II needs had necessitated rapid advances in computing for gun firing control and radar guidance. Communications were now a vital necessity in business life. Following war technical advances came the invention of the transistor in 1948 at Bell Labs. Next in rapid succession came the space race and an emerging missile and aerospace industry which utilized solid-sate designs and miniaturization requirements such as use of the transistor, plus an array of military technical advances and miniaturization in all electronic areas.

And, as examples of computer progress, the world of large mainframe computers saw the emergence of the ENIAC in 1948 [12] and the UNIVAC I, 1951.[13]

The accumulated technology advancement areas were directly falling into the realms of \the Burroughs business sectors.

Burroughs Goals and Focus

During the Coleman Era, an important line of business accounting machines were produced and upgraded. Those machines were the Sensimatic and Sensitronic lines.

The Sensimatic line came out in 1950, the Sensitronic in 1955.[14]

The Sensimatic had a moving programmable carriage to maintain ledgers. The Sensitronic could store balances on a magnetic stripe that was part of the ledger card.[15]

B-NOTE

The company name was changed from Burroughs Adding Machine Company to the Burroughs Corporation in 1953.[16]

A-NOTE

Old public habits die hard. Long, long after 1953, I was often asked about my employer, "The adding machine company?"

John Coleman had the charge of steering Burroughs through his dual period of accounting machine and computer focus maintaining earnings and also being very aware that standing still in technology would not be a survival option.

B-NOTE

Burroughs Key (No. 5) Continually invest in Research and Development

Fortunately for the Burroughs Corporation, it already had a long history of meeting specialized governmental contracts and designing beyond its adding machine general line.

What was left to Mr. Coleman, in conjunction with the appointment of Ray R. Eppert in 1956 and 1957 was to make the strategic move to acquire ElectroData Corporation of California and produce, build, and sell a computer under the Burroughs nameplate quickly and literally get in the computer game seriously.

Defense Business

The importance of being a part of the defense business was always in the Burroughs sights and Burroughs did well continuing under defense and military contracts through the Coleman Era. The big payoff in computer design was still ahead but Burroughs had done important research connected to defense in all the preceding years that was crucial for them.

Some examples were:

1955   Radar data processing equipment for SAGE (Semi-Automatic Ground   Environment[17]

1956   ATLAS (ICBM) transistorized guidance computer[18]

Significantly for Burroughs, It was under Mr. Coleman's watch that Burroughs established research and development facilities in the Philadelphia area, where much of defense and large scale computing development eventually occurred.[19]

B-NOTE

Burroughs Key (No. 6) Maximize crossover benefits from defense contracts

Acquisitions

ElectroData Corporation

After World War II, Burroughs executives faced a decision concerning the emerging electronic and computer age and how to participate.

There were two men in charge at Burroughs when the acquisition of ElectroData came to be. The primary man was still John Coleman in 1957 but Ray R. Eppert was coming to power and was working on the inside closely within Burroughs. This leadership crossover was another evidence of the value of the Burroughs philosophy of promoting insiders. That stability provided a solid background for the changing guard at Burroughs and insured everyone knowing exactly what was going on during the acquisition and why. It was an important continuum for Burroughs.

B-NOTE

Burroughs Key (No. 7) Normally promote from within for top management positions

That major in-house management continuum decision was evident in the purchase of the ElectroData Corporation plant in Pasadena, California, in 1956. When Burroughs needed to catch up fast, buying a producing plant that was doing what it needed was dictated. Burroughs already had several of its own manufacturing plants from earlier days, such as one on Tireman Road in Detroit, Michigan, and a Plymouth, Michigan, facility as well . Burroughs had been running facilities for its important banking machine and supplies business all along but it needed a competitive leap.

An analyst's view of the purchase appeared in 1961: "July, 1956, Burroughs bought ElectroData, which built general purpose electronic equipment - Datatron. The company was developed by Consolidated Electrodynamics Corporation in 1953. It did defense work – highly diversified work. Had close relationship – research defense and adaptation to commercial products.[20]

Acquiring ElectroData was one of the most important product shift advancing moves Burroughs did. ElectroData had early small computing machines that Burroughs could market such as the B205 and B250 series and later the B340 small banking machine. Other ready product examples were the line of ElectroData "Datatron" models.

Acquiring ElectroData put Burroughs front and center in the computer market with products ready to sell and thereby compete.

Other acquisitions made by Burroughs under Mr. Coleman were:

1949   Mittag & Volger, Inc, Park Ridge, New Jersey[21]

1949   Acme Carbon and Ribbon Company, Ltd., Toronto, Canada[22]

1954   Haydu Brothers, Plainfield, New Jersey, vacuum tubes and electronic components[23]

1955   Todd Company, Rochester, New York, business forms, checks, supplies[24]

Plants

The Coleman Era

The growing strength of Burroughs after WWII under John Coleman was evident in its growing population of plants in the USA and abroad.

USA plants were in place in Detroit, New Jersey, New York, Ohio, and California. Overseas plants were in England, Scotland, France and Brazil.

The Coleman Legacy

Within the ranks of the Burroughs management leaders from 1946 to 1986, all five contributed to the forward momentum of the company in their own way and style.

John Coleman set the pace and course well as was acknowledged later by Ray Macdonald who noted John Coleman supported making expenses on research and development one of the Burroughs key philosophies.

Chapter 3

The Ray R. Eppert Era (1957-1966)

The Second of the Five Final Leaders

Ray R. Eppert, the second of the final five leaders of Burroughs, was also a salesman, as was his predecessor, John Coleman. Mr. Eppert continued the tradition of sales experience being one of the common factors for most of the Burroughs management heads. He was also someone who rose through the Burroughs ranks, which was another common trait at Burroughs.

What Mr. Eppert faced as chief executive ("president" was one the various titles used by Burroughs over its history) was the continuing change of business in adding and business machines from strictly mechanical to electrically driven machines and on to the use of magnetic stripes and core storage. The changes continued on to the use of vacuum tubes and the transistor.

B-NOTE

The Burroughs titles of chief officers varied over time as they did in the rest of the business world with differing duties attached.

In 1966, Mr. Eppert was given the title of Chairman

and CEO and Ray W. Macdonald, who was waiting in the wings, was given the title of president at that time.[25]

Business Environment

The political backdrop to the period ranged from President Eisenhower's watch, through the election of John Kennedy, the devastating assassination, and on into the Johnson years.

The world scene was focused on Viet Nam and post-WWII Russian ambitions.

The American society was coincidentally moving from the relative calm and comfort of the 50's to the more radical changes of the 60's and the major contrasting Viet Nam war opinions.

This period of 1957 through 1966 was another of the continuing periods of rapid technological change going on world-wide.

Burroughs Environment

The Eppert Era carried the Burroughs Corporation through those rapid technology advances appearing in the information industry in the late 50's and early 60's and held the focus of Burroughs on the dual goals of marketing accounting and business machines plus building an associated profitable computer industry.

The big technical change going on in Mr. Eppert's rein included the vacuum tube to transistor and solid-state evolution.

During his time as chief of Burroughs, the military were purchasing solid-state designs in missile technology and other aerospace applications and it was also in this Eppert period of Burroughs history that vacuum tube computers had been built for market initially out of the ElecroData plant.

Significantly, another trend was appearing in the information business. The computer market was tough and getting tougher. Many potential players were appearing but not all were guaranteed a long-range survival.

The information marketing environment was becoming fast paced and competition was strong. Burroughs devised and continued several representative business approach indicators in the Eppert years to support both aggressive business machine and computer marketing.

These approaches included:

- Continuing a global marketing presence.
- Acquiring needed or missing expertise
- Maintaining Detroit, Michigan, as home base
- Utilizing all the company assets to their maximum

- Building on special defense design project technologies
- Designating Burroughs machine styles by the identifiable prefix of B plus three or four digits for easy product recognition
- Maintaining an aggressive approach of future development and R & D to leap-frog the competition
- Keeping a focus on current and future customer needs for market direction planning
- Keeping the already profitable successful accounting machine core business market area focused in planning.

Product Announcement Trends

Here are sample listings of various representative Burroughs products appearing in the printed media during the Eppert Era:

> A representative product introduced on 1961 that represented the Burroughs bread and butter business was the E101 desk-sized electronic digital computer. It was designed to be to be simple to use. It employed a pin-board instruction system and had an end frame utilizing 16 roles of holes. The Sensimatic was the keyboard for the E101.
>
> B5000 System announced 1961[26] (Goal: Simple

22

programming using COBOL and ALGOL)

Four new systems: B250, B260, B270, B280 from Burroughs, 1961[27]

E101 announced 1961

B5000 systems shipped 1963[28]

B200 introduced late 1963[29]

E210 arrives, 1964[30]

E2100 introduced 1964[31]

E4000 Accounting System announced, 1966[32]

A B5500 System was used for time and scoring of the Detroit Gold Cup Races, 1966[33]

B3500 systems (3) were sold and shipped 1966[34]

These representative listings show why future Burroughs leader Ray Macdonald stated in 1966 that Burroughs was in the small accounting machine business in a big way and those sales contributed substantially to the company bottom line.

Burroughs as a corporation never overlooked the importance of their profitable lower-scale products.

B-NOTE

Burroughs Key (No. 8) Maintain core business while developing future products

Burroughs Goals and Focus

Ray Eppert steered the corporation through adding and business machine expansions and kept the company's eye on the future during the intensive entrance period into the computer business world.

Two major events in Mr. Eppert's command rein were the early integrating of ElectroData Corp of California and the inception of the B5000 System design project.

ElectroData moved Burroughs into the vacuum tube based small computer markets more rapidly than Burroughs could do it. And, the B5000 System made Burroughs a technological leader.

A-NOTE

There are many insightful books and comments in the business literature about the pros and cons of acquisitions. One observation, that of Jim Collins in his book, *Good to Great*, discusses this topic well.[35]

Burroughs made many acquisitions over its lifetime. ElectroData appears to be one of those acquisitions that became a major positive component of the Burroughs story.

Later on in Mr. Eppert's leadership, the B5000 system design project produced another great leap for Burroughs.

The developmental jump to the B5000 design was to a landmark solid-state machine, one of the Burroughs' decisions that proved monumental and a fortuitous key to its future.

Mr. Eppert preceded Ray Macdonald as head of Burroughs but due to the Burroughs pattern of promoting insiders, both these executives were active on the Burroughs scene before and after their respective appointments. This pattern of overlapping management style had the benefit of smoothing out what was going on and helped transitioning between appointments because both men knew the current activities.

This fact was highly significant because this was the period of an accelerated major entry into computing for Burroughs.

B-NOTE

Significantly, the appointment of W, Michael Blumenthal as chief executive of Burroughs in 1979 was the first appointment of an "outsider" to the highest post. In fact, Mr. Paul Mirabito, chief officer at the time, stated it was because W.M.B was an outsider that he was picked. The purpose was for new "thinking" and changing the accustomed use of staffing highly-centralized management with insiders.

Defense Business

Defense contracts and specialized military projects ran through the Burroughs history with very satisfying results for Burroughs business, as noted in earlier chapters. The relationship with the military provided real experiences for research and development to blossom and the spin-off to the Burroughs knowledge-base was useful right up to the Burroughs merger with Sperry Corp to become Unisys and beyond.

During Mr. Eppert's guidance, there were three significant military projects to spotlight, in addition to many other things Burroughs did under defense contracts:

Vacuum Tube to Solid-State Projects

The Burroughs Corporation

Three defense-oriented vacuum tube computer efforts that became part of the Burroughs pool of research and development knowledge are listed on several Internet resources as important developments for Burroughs. The three machines were: the Atlas Guidance Computer, the D825, and the 2111.[36]

These three machines, described in detail on the cited *Unisys History Newsletter* by George Gray, point out the contributions by Burroughs Great Valley Research Laboratory at Paoli, Pennsylvania, for the first two designs and the efforts of a Burroughs computer development group in Pasadena, California, on the 1211 Project linked to ElectroData products.

The Atlas Guidance Computer project was an effort for the Air Force in 1959 (built at Tireman Road plant in Detroit), the D825 project was for the Navy, and the 2111 Project was an internal Burroughs effort prior to the B5000 system

Other examples of Burroughs defense contracts were one for NORAD (North American Defense Command), D825-based, in 1966[37], and the building of the Atlas Guidance Computer at the Detroit Tireman plant in 1959.[38]

The B5000 System

As mentioned previously, Burroughs under Mr. Eppert didn't stop forging ahead with the acquisition of ElectroData. It also undertook extensive R & D for the B5000 series large computer design, which was to be the leader in the corporation's direction of providing customer ease of use, multiprocessing, stack architecture, virtual memory, and a full variety of technical advances to build a future customer base with machines that would be both evolutionary and evolutionary coming from the technical experience Burroughs had been massing in special projects and acquisitions.

Therefore, for a variety of important reasons, Burroughs created the B5000 series to perform on a much larger computing scale than the smaller B200 and B300 series machines. This series was designed to lead the company's technical advances and innovative thinking into the growing computer marketplace where IBM's machines were well-established. The new series of B5000 machines would be larger, faster, and capable of greater processing power than any of the previous Burroughs offerings. It was to be an all solid-state design.

A system that easily "recognized" adding printers and tape drives was one of the technical basics of computing that Burroughs incorporated and offered to the marketplace.

The B5000 system architecture was loaded with technical ideas and features that became industry computing standards. Stack architecture, multiprocessing, multiprogramming, ease of use, virtual memory management, and a modular Master Control Program (MCP) written in a form of ALGOL were some of the technical basics of computing that Burroughs incorporated and offered to the marketplace.

B-NOTE

Burroughs Key (No. 9) Provide ease of use for customers

A-NOTE

The ease of use designed into the B5500 system was particularly evident in how the machine was cleared and restarted by the Halt/Load operation. As noted in *Modern Data*, "...the B5500 system is extremely easy to restart: Operator pushes HALT button to stop the system and the LOAD button to load a fresh version of the MCP (Master Control Program) from disk."[39]

In the early days of the young B5500 system, that operation did have a frequent need but that vastly improved later. On the lighter side, Operators of the system had to scramble to get off the system quickly if another person was coming on to use the machine. Hitting HALT/LOAD was the dreaded end to your time...no survivors.

Research and Development

To Mr. Eppert's credit, his leadership was noted in *FORBES* in an article titled, "Anatomy of a Turnaround": "Eppert …kept the R & D money flowing…allowed tech people to make the B5500".[40]

However, in a later speech in 1975, Ray Macdonald credited the earlier John Coleman as the executive who first championed the focus on research and development for Burroughs. "The decision to begin electronics research…was made by John Coleman."[41]

B-NOTE

The approval and design of the B5000 System, with its technical leaps in the industry, required many factors to come together within Burroughs for success. This project and the company's diligence produced one of Burroughs' most successful contributions and the legacies of it applied broadly across computing history.

A-NOTE

A perfect example of the B5000 design legacy came to me in 1989 when I was presented with a personal need to support and work on the Digital Equipment PDP and VAX lines.

To my surprise, I found it was like returning home to familiar ground from my Burroughs years – a most welcome realization that good design and concepts do endure. The B5000 System was one of those designs.

Fortunately, from a historical standpoint, there exists preserved at the Charles Babbage Institute at the University of Minnesota, an oral history of The Burroughs B5000 Conference of 6 September 1985, Marina del Ray, California.[42]   The Abstract of the conference says, "The Burroughs 5000 computer series is discussed by individuals responsible for its development and marketing from 1957 through the 1960s in a conference sponsored by AFIPS (American Federation of Information Processing Systems) and the Burroughs Corporation." Twenty-four pertinent conference participants are interviewed, covering three sessions concerning the technical, product development, and marketing of the system. Included in the interviews were presidents Ray Eppert and Ray Macdonald as well as designers and experts in the computing field.

Acquisitions and International Expansion

Following the Burroughs business tradition, Mr. Eppert shepherded more acquisition and international expansion in his tenure.

In the acquisition area, Strand Engineering Co. of Ann Arbor, Michigan, was acquired in 1961 (maker of displays).

On the international scene, the media reported Burroughs S/A of Oslo, Norway, was opened in 1963.[43]

Eppert's Legacies

The following comments from the media summed up Mr. Eppert's efforts during his tenure well:

In 1961, Paine, Weber, Jackson, Curtis pointed out the significance of Burroughs growth and profits through research and new ideas.

In 1996, "Mr. Eppert is generally credited with transforming Burroughs from a supplier of electro-mechanical equipment to electronic devices.[44]

"While Eppert was president, Burroughs revenue soared from $294 million in 1958 to $459 million in 1968."[45]

The Burroughs Corporation

Chapter 4.

The Ray W. Macdonald Era (1966-1976)

The Third of the Five Final Leaders

The appointment of Ray W. Macdonald to run the Burroughs Corporation following Ray R. Eppert was made using similar lines of requirements Burroughs always looked for in a chief manager. He was the third leader in the Coleman, Eppert, Macdonald, Mirabito, Blumenthal chain of the five final leaders. His imprint on Burroughs was that of a major influential figure in so many ways.

He was a salesman, as his predecessors had been. He was an insider, knew the corporation's business, and he was a reportedly a very active manager sometimes criticized by the media as being too much in control. What he did do was lead Burroughs through his tenure with a documented ability to manage the dual goals of manufacturing business machines and products as well as sell computers which left a vital company in prominence in the information field in 1977 when he stepped down.

Ray Macdonald made many key decisions during his reign that kept Burroughs on track in the competitive business of computing and a review of his era at Burroughs features several of them.

His role in Burroughs profoundly shaped the final twenty years of the company's existence. He made his mark impressively on everything Burroughs did until he was followed by Paul S. Mirabito, who acted in some ways as a bridge to the final Burroughs executive, W. Michael Blumenthal.

A-NOTE

Ray Macdonald had about ten years to shape and form Burroughs to his thinking. W. Michael Blumenthal held an additional eight year span for his management decisions regarding Burroughs. The combined influence and effect of these two men alone is the core story of Burroughs in its final years. It begins with Ray Macdonald and what he did when he stepped up in 1966. He would propel Burroughs to its heights; the man for the time.

What the Media Said

Some of the early media comments in 1966 began to draw a composite of Ray Macdonald.

An article in the *Wall Street Journal* reported, "Burroughs has a tradition of letting the president run the show." "This company has had a succession of very strong presidents,..." one

company insider said. "Mr. Macdonald is over six feet tall."
One salesman described him as a "very demanding guy".

And, "…insiders figure Mr. Macdonald will continue to
push Burroughs more heavily onto electronic data processing
equipment for offices."[46]

In 1970, "Burroughs profits and revenues for the first
quarter…28%, were highest in this period in the company's
history."[47]

And, "Ray Macdonald, president, reports record earnings
for the 6-month period 6/30/70 end: 23% over 1969."[48]

As for customer feelings, the *Wall Street Journal* reported in
1970, "Burroughs showed the highest loyalty ratio of any
manufacturer."[49]

An insightful article about the style of Burroughs was
printed in 1970 by the *Detroit Free Press*: "Burroughs
Corporation, the quietest and most self-contained company in
the frantic computer industry, joined its noisier competition this
week with a technically impressive new line of equipment."[50]

Coincident with this article, the *Wall Street Journal* printed
this announcement: "Burroughs – New Line – B700 Series –
(with) cost and performance advantages:

B5700   by December 1970

B6700   by February 1971

B7700   by early 1972[51]

Burroughs Environment

In 1966, the Burroughs Corporation and its Detroit ancestor companies were already logging more than 60 years in the business. The corporation was going into its final twenty years as a company (although it didn't know that then) with aggressive plans set and movement underway to be a major player in the new computer market.

A-NOTE

From what eventually transpired for the Burroughs Corporation, I like to refer to the last twenty years of the company as "The Great Years". All that Burroughs could become came to life in this final dual decade.

Thus, 1966 and the appointment of Ray W. Macdonald to run Burroughs is a good year to mark as a check point in the corporation's life and note what major changes were in the wind for it as well as what was happening in the country at that time.

At that time, Burroughs continued to position itself to be a player in the emerging computer age. ElectroData had been acquired in 1956; the B5000 System had been introduced in 1961. Now, Burroughs still faced playing a very competitive catch-up game and had to build a platform of research and development innovations to compete, especially in their home business of banking. Not only did they need products but they had to learn how to sell and support them.

Burroughs already had a strong legacy of manufacturing business machines as well as the production and sales of business supplies behind that. This legacy helped make it ready to take on the push into the computer business sector.

Granted, the strong and solid business legacy was there but not big or deep enough to handle the new types of business to come. The preparation for that new computer business goal was now evolving from the ground-laying efforts in the accelerating years just prior.

Major Business Statement – A New World Headquarters

There was no serious high-profile World Headquarters for Burroughs in Detroit when the Macdonald era opened. A plan for a new World Headquarters Building was in the works but it wasn't a reality yet. Negotiations with Detroit and evaluations of all options were obviously going on though, as was eventually revealed in the end of the sixties when the new headquarters was built.

The business heart of the company was still in the old, low brick building along Second Avenue that was definitely showing its age. It was probably built circa 1904 as part of the company's first presence in Detroit. To be kind, in 1966, the best part of it was the lawn along Second Avenue which was always well kept and an elegant oasis in Detroit's New Center area.

The old, low brick building had served for years as the office front for the company with the decaying old six-wing five-story adding machine plant located directly behind it on the Burroughs property. That old manufacturing plant building, which was probably built circa 1918, had seen better years. It was looking very forlorn in 1966. The purpose of the old plant to withstand heavy machinery loads was evident. It had a striking industrial structural look with exceptionally high ceilings for the overhead machinery requirements. A cafeteria was still there in 1966 but not much else.

Also in 1966, there were several corporate functions still located in the old, low brick front building, including the offices of Chairman Ray MacDonald in the higher part of the structure.

A-NOTE

As a newly-minted employee of Burroughs in 1967, I worked in that old building. So, it was not unusual to have Ray Macdonald occasionally ride up with those of us who worked on the second floor Sales Technical Services offices. He was there in the elevator, right along with us workers, but then rode on up to the mysterious administration area above. To me, Ray Macdonald really looked the part of an executive. He was tall, erect, and offered a friendly gaze. He appeared typecast for his role in the Detroit's business circles of the Sixties and a very suitable head of a corporation that was on the move. At the time, I didn't know he had recently been appointed to be the Burroughs president in 1966[52] but discovered later we both were relatively new at our jobs.

His effect on Burroughs history was a crucial and important contribution, as the following years proved.

The New World Headquarters, Detroit, Michigan

So, one of the first of many major changes made by Ray Macdonald for Burroughs came about with the building of a new World Headquarters Building. It would be a defining business statement for Burroughs and a quantum leap for its image.

The Decision

Considerations:

- Burroughs owned the site in Detroit

- Detroit was the company's historical home since 1904

- An important unfilled need existed for a major visible business presence

- A large resident employee force was working in the area

- Burroughs had other plants and business locations in the area

- Possible Incentives to build from both State of Michigan and City of Detroit

- A central Midwest location could serve both a national and international area

The decision to build was announced in the print media in late 1968.

From the *BEMA News Bulletin*:

"World Headquarters To Be Built...", announced by Ray W. Macdonald, president:

1st Phase 12/70

2nd phase 1/71

Architects: Smith & Gardner, Detroit."[53]

And, further details appeared in the *Michigan Contractor-Builder* in 1972:

"Burroughs commissioned in 1966 – Smith & Gardner Architects of Southfield - to carry out a feasibility study---to determine advantages of remaining in this strategically desirable area (New Center, Detroit).   The study showed it was practical, both physically and economically...

Phase One to be completed October 1971

Phase Two to be completed in 1972"[54]

The Location

The Macdonald Era

The land between Second and Third Avenues south of the New Center area at W. Grand Boulevard and Woodward Avenue had been the home of Burroughs for its entire existence in Michigan. Originally seed farm land at the beginning, it was now in 1967 a slightly remote urban area a few blocks from the Fisher Building and the General Motors Building in the New Center area.

The site was in a mixed-use area, sited just in from Woodward Avenue and surrounded by two expressways, small inner city streets plus railroad tracks and some undeveloped land. For employees working at the site, the service area was the New Center area and its facilities.

The location was not in downtown Detroit but in a more satellite area up Woodward Avenue north from downtown.

To the south of Burroughs was the Wayne State University Campus. Significantly, with the building of a new world headquarters building at the Burroughs site, an entire corridor of critical urban revitalization was rising from the New Center towards the inner city of downtown Detroit.

Although Burroughs had plants and did major work in Southern California technical locations, it still had an apparent strong internal impetus to maintain its presence in Detroit.

Two other desirable features of the location were the important transportation pluses of a pair of expressways crossing near the site and the location of the Detroit Metropolitan airport not too far to the west for both national and international travel access.

The Design

One important window into what Burroughs was thinking about as a future move was the decision in the 1960's to build their new World Headquarters on the site of the old five-story factory shell rotting away in its field of weeds.

The design had to make a strong statement about the corporation. It had to be suitable for and appropriate for a major player in the computer market. Most of all, it had to look substantial and as solid as its banking and manufacturing clients.

The corporation worked out tax deals and incentives with the City of Detroit and State of Michigan, had an architectural rendering made up, and announced the new home would be built.

B-NOTE

Burroughs Key (No. 10) Identify and make best use of current and past assets

The Macdonald Era

When the old factory was taken back to its very steel frame and floors in preparation for the project, it was hard to imagine what could happen there.

Creating the headquarters on the old steel frame of the five-story, six-wing factory was chosen. This decision posed special problems in scaling an office building on extra-high floor heights and floor widths designed for factory use and not offices and corridors.

The building was faced North straddling the site instead of facing it to either Second or Third Avenues. Customer demonstration areas were on the first floor by the arrival canopy. Executive offices were on the fifth floor.

The architects and the builders took the steel skeleton and cement floors of the old adding machine factory and transformed then into an elegant, classic, high-ceilinged building based on the original industrial design. The resulting look was simple, functional, clean, and proportioned appealingly over the former steel frame.

Windows were large dual panes set in pre-cast sand-colored panels that fit between each main outside vertical support girder on each floor.

The factory-based design did require extra high doors and non-standard framing in the interior spaces as well as restricting the width of some offices to fit the factory floor dimensions and the added requirements of allowing for a corridor inside each wing.

Special touches included walls of glass on the front entrance wing on the first floor and escalators from the first to second floor in the front cross-hall of the building to move people efficiently

A-NOTE

We who worked in the old brick central office building on Second Avenue while the new structure was going up often watched the changes on the site daily. The excavation phase produced a discovery of an old swimming pool there just in from Second Avenue that nobody seemed to remember was there. It could have been a perk for workers use long before health facilities popped up as a perk in business life.

(The *New Center News* in Detroit documented the pool's existence by noting in 1967: "…employee swimming pool (found) …built 55 years ago (1912))"[55]

B-NOTE

Burroughs had other perks for employee's well-being in its history. They created the Burroughs Farms

property in Brighton, Michigan, where Burroughs families and employees trekked for golf and summer cabin use for years. Few Burroughs employees missed a visit to that pleasant Michigan setting when they were in the area.

Other evidences of further employee recreational perks such as a gymnasium, a baseball team, and other recreational pursuits of a particular time period have been reported in early Burroughs history.

The World Headquarters Opens

The building opened over a period of time in 1969.

In that capacity, it signaled the corporation was an indeed serious world competitor and player, Detroit was its proud home, and quality and style were a part of its DNA.

Noteworthy, however, was the fact not all the Detroit home office associated groups were able to be housed in the new building as large as it was. Burroughs for years leased office spaces in many buildings in the New Center area for various groups that didn't need to be housed in the World Headquarters as part of their function.

A-NOTE

A special memorable elegant showing off the building occurred during the Bi-Annual CUBE (Cooperating User's of Burroughs Equipment) Detroit meeting in the fall of 1970.

The convention attendees who had come to Detroit for the Fall convention were invited to an evening cocktail affair held on the front first floor of the building in the setting of the spacious glass-walled, marble floored area designed as the general reception area and designated entry-way for product demonstration suites. Burroughs did the event in style and the building was allowed to show its very capable social side for the evening.

B-NOTE

The building is now the home of the Ford Health System at 1 Ford Place. The address was originally 1 Burroughs Place, as named when the Burroughs World Headquarters opened.

As late as the mid-eighties, Burroughs still remained committed to maintaining Detroit as its world headquarters.

Then, in the next few years when the Burroughs-Sperry merger became the main topic, the location of the headquarters of a merged Burroughs became a major speculation topic. But, under W. Michael Blumenthal in 1984, Burroughs added new office facilities at the Detroit site as noted in the *Detroit Free Press*:

"Burroughs to build $40 million office complex next to the World Headquarters by 1987. Architects are: Rossetti & Associates of Detroit."[56]

B-NOTE

The merged Burroughs-Sperry company that became Unisys in 1986 soon relocated to Blue Bell, Pennsylvania as the home location of the new company

Business Environment in 1967

Current events and social movements in America were experiencing a volatile period in activities going on and around Burroughs in 1967.

The U.S. president was Lyndon Johnson, the time was the turbulent decade of the Sixties.

George Romney was governor of Michigan. Jerome Cavanaugh was mayor of Detroit.

(Later presidents in the Macdonald era were Richard Nixon, Gerald Ford, and Jimmy Carter).

Major events in the Macdonald era included:

- The Viet Nam War
- The Detroit Riots of 1967
- Social unrest activities across America
- Changing urban and suburban patterns in many major cities

Of no small significance, 1967 was the year the City of Detroit was involved in the social riots originating on Twelfth Street, not very far from the Burroughs site. The center of the riot scene was within blocks of the Burroughs Second Avenue location. Even closer to Burroughs, selected business property damage was done along Woodward Avenue south of West Grand Boulevard which was very close to the Burroughs front door.

The events that July were momentous and carried deep meaning and implications for the city and Burroughs. Almost unimaginable earlier, a rare military presence was on Woodward Avenue and still there in plain sight when Burroughs was able to resume business activities.

The Macdonald Era

The Detroit riots were just prior to the new World Headquarters being built. This fact alone is an important footnote into the thinking and planning of Burroughs as they decided to position their world headquarters on the Detroit site. Although the announcement of the new world headquarters had been made earlier in 1966, by both Ray Eppert and Ray Macdonald, the obvious financial considerations were important but so was the Burroughs resolve when it made the statement of putting a world-class building and its headquarters steps away from what became a very recent major social-upheaval event.

Macdonald's Goals and Plans

In a revealing media piece Ray Macdonald in 1970, the *Detroit News* printed an article titled, "Burroughs: A Super Salesman Pushes The Buttons". In this article, the paper pointed out computers were only 6% of Burroughs 1970 sales.[57] And, the paper also pointed out that Burroughs, Honeywell, NCR, GE, Control Data, UNIVAC and others made up only 30% of the 1970 computer market.[58]

Assets in 1967

Burroughs had a successful business machine and financial supply business going.

Burroughs had the old brick building and the decaying three-wing, five-story factory building on its New Center area site near W. Grand Boulevard in Detroit.

It owned several plants that made banking and business supplies.

It owned the Burroughs Farms golf course and resort in Brighton, Michigan, a family perk for employees.

It had an on-going military defense provider presence in Paoli, Pennsylvania.

It had the Pasadena, California plant, the former ElectroData Corporation computer manufacturer acquired in 1957. This was the source for the DATATRON computers and the Burroughs B220 line.

A sales force was already in place serving mainly the banking, accounting and financial industries built on its adding machines and calculating products.

Macdonald's Business Focus

Burroughs was a manufacturer and marketer of calculators, adding machines, business supplies and evolving early computer machines.

The company was moving from these adding machines and other business machines to computers and had the dual major task of training former adding machine sales people to support and market new high tech computing products. The sales force continued selling its original business lines but now had to be able to grow computer-oriented users. This need created a significant training requirement for the sales force that Burroughs had to provide.

The migration from mechanical machines to high-tech hardware and software focus was no small challenge to Burroughs. They were tackling this issue aggressively.

Attitude, Approaches, and Business Style

Burroughs ran lean, had an important technical developmental past, had many assets that could be used or modified, had a large site in Detroit's New Center area, and had a strong vision of where it wanted to go.

There was an obvious attitude within the company to compete and compete hard. Changes were in the wind and Burroughs was intent on being a major player in what was coming. The pieces were being put in place to do just that, with products, Research and Development, and new employee additions to get there. That was all part of the approach going on.

In the old main office building, Burroughs was already pushing the hiring envelope. They selected talented women and minorities to be part of the new information system teams. Burroughs overlooked little in being ready the best way they could. They weren't lowering standards to do it. To be an employee in many technical positions of the company, an engineering or sciences undergraduate degree was necessary. Burroughs wanted to be a serious player and was going for it right from the start.

B-NOTE

Burroughs Key (No. 11) Employ diversity in employee hiring

Also, due to the leanness of staffing, each employee was counted on to produce and learn fast – a point that became almost a "family" pride.

One of the greatest things about working at Burroughs was how lean they worked and how soon an employee got the mandate to dig in and produce results. There weren't large "groups" or several layers to impede an employee. For instance, in the technical documentation department, where manuals were created, the technical writer went to a single resource person often (or at least a very few) for information on the product and worked directly with them to produce the operating manual.

That sense of being in on things and being given a lot of personal responsibility was absorbed into most in the Burroughs employee family and that produced some fierce loyalty.

That mandate to learn and produce fast with responsibility had a parallel in the military

where major efforts are done with young and raw recruits tied to experienced mentors.

Burroughs either borrowed that concept or employed on its own due to pure financial considerations. It worked.

B-NOTE

Burroughs Key (No. 12) Run lean and delegate high responsibility

A-NOTE

Running lean had a humorous side, too. When I was doing Large Systems COBOL customer compiler problem support in Sales Technical Services in Detroit forwarding validated problems to the designers in California, someone once asked me how my group was doing? There was no "group". I was it. So, I reported the group was doing just fine!

A-NOTE

In 1967, I joined Burroughs as a technical writer and worked in the documentation department in the Sales Technical Services (STS) group on the second floor of the old brick office building. STS was the technical support group interfacing with the customers' software and hardware support needs and sales support needs with the product designers in the plant.

Products at that time included the B5500 computer system and several smaller machines specifically targeted for banking, such as the B340 computer and other B200 series machines. Supported software languages were mainly COBOL, FORTRAN, and ALGOL, as well as some specialized software programs Burroughs was marketing for specific users of their computing products.

B-NOTE

An example of Burroughs "lean" structure, the instruction technical manual for the B340 Small Computer was produced by one technical writer and the documentation team using technical information from one product information person. This lean style made close, fast, turnaround time and eliminated layers of possible error in between. All the participants for the manual were in the old brick two-story Burroughs

building on Second Avenue. That tight concept showed up in later business lore as "group" task forces, cutting through separate department structures to produce quality results.

Products - Hardware

In 1967, the products Burroughs had out on the market included the dual mix of electronic business machines as well as computers, which would be the standard mix for Burroughs later down the line. For computers, Burroughs had the B200 series and B340 small banking machines coming out of the Pasadena plant and the technically advanced B5000/B5500 large-scale machines on the market. The B5500 large-scale design, with the revolutionary MCP (Master Control Program) Operating System, was a Burroughs advance point design for future products.

Macdonald shepherded huge technical product line expansions during his era such as offering the B5500 and later the B5700 and then later the B5900. Expansion and offerings like these across the Burroughs machine series were coming out routinely from Macdonald's Burroughs.

Other revenue products in their stable included continuing those government defense projects and continuing their bread-and-butter business as a general supplies resource for the banking and accounting industry.

Many innovative computing ideas and machines also came out of the Macdonald era.

To Ray Macdonald's credit, this kind of technical leadership came out of this chairman who at first admittedly focused on small business and accounting machines for their earning power. In 1967, *Business Week* had an article titled: "Ray Macdonald lukewarm views about the company's efforts in computers?"[59]

If nothing else, he obviously changed with the times, adapted, and led.

During Macdonald's tenure, new hardware announcements continually rolled out of Burroughs for sales.

In 1970, the *Wall Street Journal* printed:

"Burroughs new family of machines announced:

B5700, 12/70 delivery

B6700, 2/71 delivery

B7700, early 1972 delivery

The machines were designed for: Very large databases, flexibility, efficiency in data communications and remote computing."[60]

In the medium systems range, the *Wall Street Journal* also reported in 1970, "Burroughs Announces B4500."[61]

And, in the small machine area, *Information Week* reported, "Burroughs announces E8000 Electronic Accounting System, running with COBOL compiled on any B3500,"[62]

All through the Macdonald era, product announcements kept coming out.

In 1966, F3000 accounting machine announced 2/14/66. Also, E4000 System 5/16/66.

In 1973, "Burroughs Announces B2700, B3700, B4700"[63]

In 1975, "Burroughs Announces 800 Series' B2800, B3800, B4800"[64]

In 1975, "L9300, L9400, L9500 business minicomputers"

In 1979, Burroughs introduced an unusual dual processor B6800 machine that could be built with Global Memory (shareable by two processors) and be split by software commands into various operating groups with processors linked together, or separate, or configured in different ways with the memory for the user's needs at any time during the processing day for changing loads.

This allowed the user of a two or more processor system to reconfigure or split their system by software control to become a variety of combinations of memory and processor power over the business day.[65]

A-NOTE

I was fortunate to get on a systems team selected to introduce the B6800 Global System to the Burroughs people via in-depth technical presentations. I have to admit it was a treat to see the system demonstrated to us in the Mission Viejo plant and even more than that, the demo worked perfectly, which is always a plus in the computing business.   The processors split into two distinct systems perfectly on command as specified.

Products - Software

Along with the aggressive introductions of computers of continually advanced design, Ray Macdonald's Burroughs was also producing major changes and offerings in its stable of software to use on them

Early software support included ALGOL, FORTRAN and COBOL among other languages popular at the time. But Burroughs remained tuned and responsive to what it was hearing from customers concerning products they needed. The CUBE bi-annual user conventions played a big part in this communication exchange as well as information gleaned from

Burroughs vendor-customer status meetings held routinely at the customers' sites.

B-NOTE

Burroughs Key (No. 13) Maintain two-way customer communications

Burroughs also focused on specialized software such as Data Communications methods to link users into computing machines. They focused on how to create large protected databases. These offerings were important departments in addition to the then popular software languages

One of their notable products in data communications to mainframes was the GEMCOS (Generalized Message Control System) of 1976. This software system utilized TCL (Terminal Control Language) to define the custom network the software generated for the user. Like many products in the Burroughs domain, this product came out of specialized technical work at a branch; in this case, Lansing, Michigan. The resulting product was based on the efforts of Burroughs specialized technical representative work there on large data communications sites in the branch.

B-NOTE

Burroughs Key (No. 14) Produce code-generating software

Another Burroughs software product that proved very useful in the large systems environment was SPARK (System Performance Analyzer Review Kit). This software allowed operators and systems staff to spot-check how the Processor, Input-Output, Memory and the Operating Mix were performing by software snapshots which produced displays, reports and histograms. The system was designed to allow a custom set-up to serve the local needs of the user via the Sampler and SAMPLEANALYZER software.

With this feature, possible "slow-downs" or unusual performance problems popping up could be checked and appropriate changes to the operating mix made for relief. It was the kind of information that helped the user be on top of things and manage the system.

DMSII

DMSII was a re-engineered and much improved data-base system that Burroughs marketed in the 1970's for the surfacing sophisticated needs of its many users. Customers required fast data-base handling, in large amounts, with guaranteed recovery and ease of programming for their many user programs.

DMSII, which followed earlier Burroughs database products, became widely used and along the line produced many technical experts both within and outside Burroughs who knew the product and could support it. One spin-off company, Joseph and Cogan, came out of its founders Chicago experiences.

Outsourcing

During the Macdonald era, the use of "outsourcing" technical support needs to a participant organization outside of Burroughs was found useful to bring added support into projects, supplement sudden new large-scale requirements, and control costs.

TATA of India was one such organization. It could be contracted to help support software conversions and similar short-range projects for a user. Being stationed in India offered off-shore cost considerations.

B-NOTE

Burroughs Key (No. 15) Utilize "Outsourcing" to supplement needs

Acquisitions

Under Macdonald, Burroughs continued to make acquisitions. As the *Buffalo Evening News* reported: In the 1970's, Burroughs acquired REDACTRON Corporation; word/processing, Graphic Sciences; facsimile devices, and Context Corporation, optical reading."[66]

Plants and Expansion

The Macdonald era saw great physical plant expansion from Burroughs. His years were the payoff time for all that had gone before in Burroughs.

Southern California featured much of the expansion. Plants were operating in Mission Viejo (1970). There were plants in Santa Barbara, Pasadena, City of Industry. Another plant appeared in Westlake Village.

In 1969, a plant was announced for Pompano Beach, FL.

In New Jersey, the Piscataway Plant was operating in 1979 for the Defense, Space and Special Systems Group.

Great Britain also saw plant expansion. One was announced for Glenrothes, Scotland, in 1969.[67]

Defense Business

The Macdonald Era

All through the Macdonald tenure, Burroughs continued to work on defense contracts through its Defense, Space and Special Systems Group. This group grew to be a separate group from the other domestic line-of-business marketing areas under the Business Machines Group.

One example of their activity was an order cited in 1969 in the *Communications News*: "Air Force buys B3500 for 150 bases in the world."[68]

Another example from 1969 is the citing of a "...Burroughs contract with Martin-Marietta Corp for 36 D84 computers for the Army Pershing 2A missile system."[69]

Bumps in the Road

As in any business, not all projects were produced without incident.

At Burroughs, as the *Kansas City Star* reported in 1970, "TWA filed a $70 million suit – alleging – misrepresentation and breach of contract. Burroughs countered for $11.5 million owed...on an automated passenger reservation and management system (B8300).[70]

Later, in 1972, the *Wall Street Journal* reported: "TWA settlement – cost $.26 a share in net and Burroughs assumes obligations regarding equipment leased TWA…a $4.8 million charge after taxes."[71]

And, not all delivery and product plans were exempt from the media scrutiny. In 1971, "Word of software problems spread through the financial community…Burroughs confirmed that there were developmental delays. The B6500, in particular, is vulnerable to delay because it offers several advanced features:

- Multiprogramming
- MCP featuring dynamic resource allocation
- Uses virtual memory
- Dual processors"[72]

What Macdonald Thought

Two reports made of what Mr. Macdonald thought (taken over nine years apart) show his range (and change) during his tenure as Burroughs management head in his own words.

The first report is from 1966 when he was at the beginning of his chief position. The article, in *FORBES*, was titled: "Burroughs Corporation: Sophisticated Buggy Whips".

"(January, 1966) Ray Macdonald was named president of Detroit's Burroughs Corporation, succeeding Ray E. Eppert, Burroughs boss since 1958.

"Burroughs," he (Macdonald) told *FORBES*, "is one of the least understood big companies around." His job? "to set the record straight."

"Computers," he says, "are no more than an attractive addition to our main business, not a replacement for it."

"Ray Macdonald is concerned that too many people judge Burroughs by its progress – or its problems – in big computers."

"Computers are the glamour business these days…but it makes up only about 10% of our revenue."

"Burroughs' revenue…is built on ordinary accounting machines…"ordinary" is not quite the right word. Accounting machines, 1966 style, are increasingly sophisticated pieces of equipment. They incorporate…memory cores…built so they can communicate with computers. They are in many ways, junior computers.

Examples are:

E1000/E1100

E2000/E2100

For the next 20 years, at least…these kinds of products will be Burroughs most important market.

He (Macdonald) concedes readily that the computer market will continue to grow more rapidly (15%-20%) a year) than the market for accounting machines.

He plans to continue spending money...Burroughs conceded it has some of the best hardware on the market, its B5500 computer first to use multi-processing."[73]

Macdonald Thoughts - 1975

The second report of Mr. Macdonald thoughts quoted here was made in 1975 when he gave a lecture at the University of Michigan Graduate School of Business Administration. The occasion was his speech entitled "The Transition of Burroughs" which was given upon receipt of his 1975 Business Leadership Award.

In this summing-up lecture, he mentioned, "The very strong position we enjoy today can be traced to pioneering decisions made by our management in the late 1940's, the effectiveness of major actions taken during two critical years in the middle 1960's, and fundamentally to the increasing professionalism of our management.

The decision to begin electronics research...was made by John Coleman.

The Macdonald Era

In 1964, "the Profit Improvement Committee", a reorganization team, had the…primary charge… the swift improvement of the company's profitability…our problems lay in the efficiency of our operations rather than in the spending levels associated with R & D."[74]

Macdonald's Position at Era's End - The Handoff To Paul Mirabito

By 1977, the information systems market was continuing to change and evolve but Ray W. Macdonald had brought Burroughs to a commanding place in the picture.

His style was frequently questioned in the media forum and even the Burroughs entire management structure was questioned as to whether it was effective or not.

But, Burroughs had kept up by most accounts knowing the sources of general revenues were changing from only business machine leases and sales to much more emphasis on software solutions and changing customer support requirements in both engineering and systems support. The trend was for standardization usage and less need for on-site specialized attention by representatives.

The machines were lasting longer, required less attention, and previous software support requirements were being reexamined to produce a revised billing scheme that better represented possible income areas and changing required expenditures in support.

The Macdonald Era

The Burroughs Corporation

Model No. 6 Adding Machine Chassis

Photo courtesy of the Charles Babbage Institute, University of
Minnesota, Minneapolis

Style No. 3 Electric Adding Machine

Photo courtesy of the Charles Babbage Institute, University of
Minnesota, Minneapolis

The Burroughs Corporation

Burroughs Detroit Facility – 1925

Photo courtesy of the Charles Babbage Institute, University of
Minnesota, Minneapolis

Norden Bombsight – WWII

Photo courtesy of the Charles Babbage Institute, University of Minnesota, Minneapolis

The Burroughs Corporation

B2000 Display at ElectroData Division – 1966

Photo courtesy of the Charles Babbage Institute, University of
Minnesota, Minneapolis

F6500 Accounting Machine

Photo courtesy of the Charles Babbage Institute, University of
Minnesota, Minneapolis

The Burroughs Corporation

B220 Computer Systems Installation – 1960

Photo courtesy of the Charles Babbage Institute, University of
Minnesota, Minneapolis

B90 System

Photo courtesy of the Charles Babbage Institute, University of
Minnesota, Minneapolis

The Burroughs Corporation

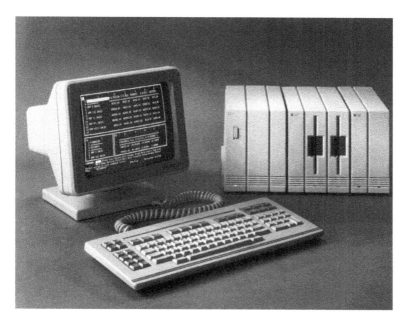

B20 Modular Terminal & CPU

Photo courtesy of the Charles Babbage Institute, University of
Minnesota, Minneapolis

B7700 Computer System

Photo courtesy of the Charles Babbage Institute, University of
Minnesota, Minneapolis

The Burroughs Corporation

A9 Computer System

Photo courtesy of the Charles Babbage Institute, University of
Minnesota, Minneapolis

Chapter 5

The Macdonald Era (1966-1976)

Life Inside Burroughs – Sales Technical Services – Central
Support - Detroit (1967-1973)

Sales Technical Services (STS) was the central technical support
group located in the old Second Avenue office building
Burroughs called home in Detroit in 1967. It was housed on the
second floor of that old building and had the assignment of
providing Burroughs centralized technical support for existing
computer lines being marketed and the software products being
sold to support them. STS also had the Documentation Group of
technical writers to produce the reference manuals needed for
both the hardware and software products.

Sales Technical Services in 1967 was a good place to view
how Burroughs was approaching the need to support its new
technical products starting to appear in their marketing area. The
new computing products required detailed information on how to
use them and a timely means to deal with problems customers
found while using them.

Through the STS area, Burroughs had created a means of
supplying necessary technical support to its growing computer
user base and, of equal importance, to its own technical employee

force. This information support was crucially important to help the users and Burroughs employees understand and use the increasingly complex computer products.

Life inside Burroughs then in STS – Detroit from 1967 to 1973 is described here from both the standpoint of the Documentation Group (1967-1970) and then the Large Systems Technical Support Group (1970-1973).

A-NOTE

Both the documentation and the computer systems technical support areas are featured and described here because I started out with Burroughs as a technical writer in 1967 until 1970 and then progressed to large systems technical support in 1970 by completing a BS-EE degree, which was one of the required scientific backgrounds for technical support in Burroughs.

Because of my work presence in these two Burroughs areas, this chapter features the Documentation Group view from 1967 to 1970 and then the Large Systems Technical Support part of Sales Technical Services from 1970-1973.

First up is the documentation technical writing period (1967-1970).

Sales Technical Services (STS) Documentation Support (1967-1970)

In 1967, Burroughs had two technical writing jobs available when I was looking for employment. Their first job was in a group that produced brochures and sales materials. That group was located in an old factory building on Holbrook, just north of the Burroughs main site on Second Avenue. The offices there were certainly modest and indicative to me of a company perhaps on the brink of expansion but certainly not there yet.

These offices were in a well-worn building designed for factory and warehouse use in a much earlier Detroit era.

The second available Burroughs job was a technical writing job producing reference manuals for the current Burroughs hardware and software products. That job was located in the old Burroughs main office building and had the added feature of being located in the same building with the STS technical systems support staff. In the blossoming computer sales effort going on then at Burroughs, being there in this second job turned out to be right in the middle of high activity and energy coming out of STS.

A-NOTE

I was hired into the STS Documentation Group in spring 1967.

What Was Going On in the USA (1967-1970)

In 1967, the Johnson presidency was to end with the election of 1968. Richard M. Nixon became president for his first term.

The Viet Nam War was in the forefront of American concerns and the social unrest of the 60's coupled with a major shift in social values were dominating the culture.

A-NOTE

The social unrest and war feelings came directly into my Burroughs life twice. First, with the closing of the Burroughs main offices briefly in the summer of 1967 due to the Detroit Riots and then later when I was reluctantly exposed to smoke-bomb protests and in-class protest confrontations at the University of Michigan Ann Arbor campus in 1969 where I was finishing a BS-EE degree for a Burroughs career change.

Both of these events pinpointed how deeply change was occurring in the country but the closeness of the Detroit Riots of 1967 to the Burroughs home site was especially significant in its history.

The Burroughs Corporation

What Was Going on in Burroughs (1967-1970)

In 1967, Burroughs was rapidly moving ahead into computers via both the small B200/B300 series of machines out of ElectroData as well as making the bigger leap into large systems spearheaded by the B5500. This transition period covered both vacuum tube products and solid-state machines, making it one of the more important evolutionary changes in the business.

Language support necessarily featured ALGOL, due to the ALGOL-based operating system for the new large systems machines, and FORTRAN – a popular language of the day, and COBOL, the language of government contracts and the banking world.

Accompanying Burroughs software applications were therefore being produced for this machine environment.

At this same time, Mr. Macdonald kept Burroughs on a straight path producing its financially rewarding business and accounting machine products and business supplies.

In STS back then, as an indicator of Burroughs' hiring diversity, talented women in technical positions were already part of that Burroughs technical support team in 1967 in Detroit.

Burroughs continued employing women in its many significant employee positions. In 1980, the Piqua Ohio *Call* noted: "At Burroughs, in 1978, total number of women in the sales force was 21%, up from 14% in 1976. 1979; even higher".[75]

Life in the Documentation Group

Reference and user information manuals being produced by the STS Documentation Group in 1967 covered relatively few early Burroughs machines.

Table B of this book mentions some of the representative products worked on then. The B340 Reference Manual was one (the B340 was a small banking machine). The B5500 Handbook (an easy to carry pocket-sized reference manual) was another. The B5500 Extended ALGOL Reference Manual and B5500 FORTRAN Compiler Reference Manual were typical of the languages. COBOL information was also produced.

Other kinds of manuals mentioned in Table B are the B300/500/5500 Audio Response System manual and the BIPS-1 Integer Programming System manual, which are examples of instructions for Burroughs special features and products.. The later-released B6500 documentation began to come out in 1969 as part of the new product introduction scheduling.

Technical writing for computers was somewhat specialized in that computer languages had computer language syntax definitions in many manuals. These syntax lines defined the language usage and had to be correct in every way.

The Documentation Group there in STS wasn't very large, which was typical of those early Burroughs departments. That small group of about six by its very nature gave major opportunities for the writers to work directly with the support technical analysts responsible for each product.

By 1970, when I moved on to Large Systems Technical Support, the Documentation Group had become a close-knit department within itself and along with most of the rest of STS as well. That closeness resembling almost an extended family style was typical of the Burroughs environment at the time and a key factor in the high employee loyally Burroughs enjoyed.

Sales Technical Services (STS) Large Systems Technical Support, Detroit (1970-1873)

Large System Technical Support Center (STS) duties in 1970 included software and hardware problem reporting, problem resolution, and production of major software releases to the Field. These software releases included tapes, documentation, and installation notes for customer use in installing and upgrading to the new release. Moving to a new release level was encouraged by Burroughs so users could take advantage of all the latest problem fixes and new features as well as to help make technical support more effective.

Software fixes (or patches) were sent out routinely from STS when problems were discovered and were resolved. Problems usually came through STS, were verified, and then sent on to plant designers. At the same time, analysts were improving the product in the plants. When enough new features were collected to improve an operating system, those new features and all the fixes to date were rolled into a new software release. The release files and documentation were sent on then to the customer base as tapes and printed information.

As well as supporting expanding hardware lines and preparing for new ones being produced routinely, Burroughs focused on and addressed other surfacing issues in the computing market that often included resources in the STS area :

1. More emphasis on total solutions for the customer. Burroughs made it a point to find ways to provide products for all of the user's information center needs

2. Provision of code to customers for their in-house modification purposes. This benefit was relatively rare in the business but by providing machine code, Burroughs allowed their users a way to insert their own features easily and customize their operations.

3. Information flow to customers continued via the CUBE conventions and product releases. Burroughs depended on listening to their customer base via conferences and scheduled status meetings at the customer.

4. The technical support structure was necessarily growing to service the needs of the new business. This was a major expansion time in Burroughs and many people were entering the computer business to provide for the growth and responses needed.

The Burroughs Corporation

On the personnel front, Burroughs faced exploring how to maximize the use of technical personnel across the entire customer field instead of continuing their earlier practice of placing costly personnel at key sites. Early requirements agreed upon to win contracts often mandated putting technical people into customer sites. But, this practice was very costly and better performance of both hardware and software was allowing the possibility of changing this arrangement to more universal and effective support thinking.

At STS, central technical support for the B5500/B5700 large computer line and its software products was now joined by the newly added B6500/B6700 support activities.

As an instance of how fast growth was surfacing at Burroughs, the company also faced other expansion problems due to the need to find suitable work space for all the growing personnel it needed. The opening of the World Headquarters building in 1970 soon filled all that newly available building space.

The continuing need for locating peripheral groups like STS in suitable offices in the Detroit area caused STS Large System Support, which was originally on the second floor of the old Second Avenue building, to move to The Wayne State Building on W. Grand Boulevard, and then move B5700 support eventually into the new World Headquarters by 1973.

What Was Going On in the USA (1970-1973)

Sales Technical Services

This period contained the end of the Nixon years, the Viet-Nam War, and the Universal Draft. It continued to be a volatile time in the country in both government and business.

What Was Going On in Burroughs (1970-1973)

Large system and medium system sites were exploding in sales. A major emphasis on and demand for large main frames and COBOL (Common Business Oriented Language) programming was in effect in both the government and business worlds. The large movement towards COBOL made its availability in contracts a must for computer manufacturers.

Larger and more robust, reliable computer systems were in demand. New design-associated machine style offerings in the Small and Medium ranges were coming to market under the general B1000/B2000/B3000/B4000/B5000/B6000/B7000 plan.

These needs fueled a move to developing support and expertise for:

- Increased up-time
- Increased data security
- Greater reliability
- Rapid and effective recovery
- Large supportable data-bases
- Sophisticated data communications ability in/out

The Burroughs Corporation

B-NOTE

Burroughs Key (No. 16) Specialize in large scale and critical businesses

B-NOTE

Burroughs Key (No. 17) Provide total solutions for customers

Life in Customer Technical Support

Many of us in Customer Technical Support in STS had duties in 1970 very similar to a combination of what is now known as the "Help Desk" service of computer companies and the Customer Service department functions for problem resolution and fixes.

Typically, problems were called in or sent in from Burroughs representatives and customer site personnel.

The problems were analyzed, duplicated and verified or checked as possible user errors. The identified problems were then forwarded to the design engineers in the appropriate plant.

In 1970, large systems problems went to the Burroughs Pasadena plant. Later, the Mission Viejo plant came on-line for large systems.

Fixes or "get-arounds" were created and sent back for handling and eventually would appear included in a major release.

The work was interesting, challenging, and required strong logic and trouble-shooting skills as well as a good presence on the phone for fact gathering.

A-NOTE

Jobs like product support are fast-paced learning situations. The tools are relevant reference manuals, the appropriate compiler printout listing, careful machine testing and verifying, and good rapport with the design engineers.

One assignment I enjoyed was supporting the COBOL compiler on large systems. That product was in major use across most computing sites due to the government requirements for it in contracts and the banking industry's favoring of it.

Perhaps not one of the more elegant computing languages, but COBOL was a business language and very much in demand out in the Burroughs user world.

The Burroughs Corporation

Chapter 6

The Macdonald Era (1966-1976)

Life Inside Burroughs – The Chicago District (1973-1976)

The Chicago District was one of the very active customer centers in the Burroughs marketing structure in 1973. By location and size alone, it was one of the big Burroughs districts, with auxiliary branches sufficient to cover the business territory. The District had a full representation of the Burroughs "Lines of Businesses" with customers in all categories, many of whom were easily recognized household names.

A major banking institution customer was Harris Trust in the Loop, The Libby, Libby, Libby brand under Nestle ownership was another representative of businesses in the Loop. Keebler Biscuit was a well-known name in the suburbs. Quaker Oats was a customer as was Abbott Labs. The list was impressively long.

In the western area, Northern Illinois Gas (NIGAS) was a large utility for Burroughs and The University of Chicago Hospital had a system then, too.

Although the various Burroughs branches represented and covered specific functions and services of the Chicago District, the district office itself was there downtown right in the heart of

95

things and held a major presence on S. Michigan Avenue with offices and a demo area on the first floor at that location.

Customer Installation Support

The Chicago District had customer installations operating in all phases of the customer support life cycle all the computer manufacturers had to address. A quick look at that support cycle helps define what the district was doing under the Burroughs nameplate.

The Customer Support Cycle

Resources had to be assigned to work on all the specific phases listed here.

The basic support cycle included:

- Pre-Sales and Proposal phases
- Benchmarks, available solutions and planning
- Conversion and software "patching" to accommodate user software
- Installation phase
- Going Live
- On-Going Support
    - Hardware and software problem resolution and fixes
    - New releases and information flow

- o Status meetings and communications
- o Support for anticipated expansion needs

Chicago Business Conditions (1973-1976)

In 1973 through 1976, Illinois was dealing with extremely high interest rates. Rates were so high they were hitting a state-instituted cap which functionally stopped home mortgage sales and a lot more.

The country was finally coming out of the Viet Nam war and the mandatory draft ended. It was also in this period the resigned presidency of Richard M. Nixon was followed by Gerald R. Ford.

Burroughs customers were concerned about the computing issues of: very large database management, large transaction rates and speeds, recovery from system crashes, data integrity and security concerns, maximum up-time guarantees and the important evaluation of whether to upgrade to new software releases for their new features and support or hold-off due to their site needs to modify new software to fit their systems.

Harris Trust Bank

A-NOTE

My first introduction into Chicago customer support was to be assigned in 1973 as a group leader in the Harris Trust Bank offices. Five of us Burroughs employees were stationed in the bank, which was a

major customer using both Medium and Large
Burroughs Systems.

As the group leader, I had the site technical systems
support responsibility and also the vendor's systems
seat at the status meetings held by bank Operations.
The four other Burroughs staff members with me
covered the specialized computer support needs of the
bank.

B-NOTE

This installation in 1973 was in the "on-going" phase of
customer support. But, as a very large size installation,
it continued to do forward planning on a very serious
basis.

The Burroughs Corporation provided our in-house
software support to this customer as part of filling the
customer's needs fully, but they also did so realizing
this customer modified its software and had a large
critical installation to maintain.

Financially, computer corporations wanted to migrate
their support staff out of sites to more centralized (and
less costly) support centers but Burroughs did at that
time what it felt necessary to service its big users.

Northern Illinois Gas Company (NIGAS)

This installation near Napierville was also an example of a user who was in the "on-going" support phase of customer-Burroughs life. They had already been assisted through installation and had become a large data-base user when they had the need in 1975 to look at the possibility of going to a more powerful new Burroughs system.

This planning required the need for information on expected through-put times, size of storage capacity, and performance that could be expected in a bigger machine. NIGAS was a system with high-volume transaction rates and huge storage requirements. Those needs dictated going to the "benchmark" phase of an installation, when there would be a trial on a representative Burroughs machine to help make the decision to go forward with a Burroughs upgrade.

The most available and closest machine to do the benchmark turned out to be in Detroit at the World Headquarters. That meant that as part of system support at the account at that time, I was going back to Detroit with the NIGAS technical staff for the benchmark. I was very pleased about that and was more than glad to have this test held in my old stomping ground.

A-NOTE

Doing the work for a benchmark is often done in the wee hours of the night because of better availability of resources. One part of hosting a customer technical team at a benchmark is for us with Burroughs to help them settle in and give them a hand with accommodations and dining.

For a start, on this trip, we went as a team to Detroit's London Chop House the first night, as a representative area restaurant for the team to enjoy. With the customer team coming from the Chicago area, I felt a certain need to showcase Detroit to the customer team in the best light. They had already made comments about the two cities prior.

The restaurant worked out well as a first choice but I felt the team wasn't bonding yet.

Work on a benchmark is challenging and stressful. With that thought in mind, I decided to take them to Buddy's Pizza on Conant Avenue the second night. I figured it was perhaps a risk but so many of us who worked in Detroit had made our way to this legendary place and enjoyed it so much. I decided it was worth the chance.

The team loved it. It was great place to have fun, talk, unwind, and just kick back eating in one of Detroit's best pizza challenges to Chicago. I think the team bonded, at least it certainly sounded like it.

Total District Team Support

As in all Burroughs installations, the Chicago District supported the customers with the requisite trio of Sales, Field Engineering, and Systems Representatives. This was the case for most computer vendors. What differed was in how many resources were allocated to customers and how they were distributed among the other users.

Burroughs had to be on the side of extra value-added simply because of the intense competition. One way this need was met was by the creation of specialists in high needs areas such as performance, high through-put and large data communications sites, and advanced data-base management installations.

Chicago was a leading market for Burroughs in data-base specialization particularly, and a few technical talents there even spun off their abilities to create a data-base support company catering to Burroughs users. That company, Joseph and Cogan, eventually became linked with Burroughs.

A similar emergence of specialized data-communications expertise formed in the Lansing Michigan Branch regarding the GEMCOS data-communications software which is mentioned later.

With the use of these specialists, the Burroughs teams often became very integrated with the customer talent and produced some impressive results.

Scheduled status meetings between Burroughs and a user were critical to keeping the communication lines open. In the Chicago District, these meetings were most important. Competition was high, technical advances were crucial to know about, and problems had to be solved rapidly.

Being invited into corporate settings for information topics gave Burroughs personnel valuable insight into how different corporations and institutions worked. The styles varied as much as the industries represented. That exposure benefited the support situation and helped in the adaptability of Burroughs to meet the customer's need.

The experiences of Burroughs employees being in corporate halls also contributed to the ability of the Burroughs central support offices (MSC-Detroit) to help other companies later by performing company information system audits.

Technical Support History

Because of the Chicago District's long history of Burroughs products use, users were encouraged to upgrade both their hardware and software to be able to use the latest fixes and features in both. Time and money dictated how long a manufacturer could fully support a software release or a machine style. Some machines in the Chicago District were serving long and well beyond the expected limits.

The Chicago District had the luxury of having employees who had worked on the very early Burroughs products and were still employed (and could be called on in an emergency) to provide their expertise on older machine problems.

B-NOTE

In one instance, Burroughs had installed and supported an early B5500 machine in a Chicago banking site for a number of years prior to 1974. A need arose for B5500/B5700 field engineering attention at the site and a search went out across the district and Illinois environs to find knowledgeable field engineering technicians to work on the machine.

A-NOTE

Burroughs found a group of senior field engineers and brought them to Chicago for the problem. While the engineers were on a break discussing the good old days, which in computing terms is not that far back, they brought up an old war story of how an ornery early B5500 machine was encouraged to run. It seems nothing worked to get the machine to load its operating system until one engineer supposedly placed a strong hand hand-slap at a crucial place on the main frame. Where to slap it was most critical, it seemed.

Additional and Unexpected Benefits of the Chicago Information Scene

Computer vendors like Burroughs had special links and experiences with an amazing array of customer situations in the Chicago area that included:

1. Being invited into the customer's environment and working with their personnel.

2. Hearing and seeing how various corporations and staffs worked on their daily problems and information system issues both on daily visiting basis and at more formal status meetings.

3. Exposure to the business workings of a wide variety of business and enterprises, both large and small, of which many were household names.

4. Opportunities to work on cutting-edge challenges that a high-energy area like Chicago generates.

5. And, opportunities to work with customer technical employees who migrated to Burroughs in the Chicago environment.

Chapter 7

The Paul S. Mirabito Era (1977-1979)

The Fourth of the Five Final Leaders

Paul S. Mirabito, the fourth leader in the last forty years of
Burroughs history, had a much more abbreviated tenure compared
to the other leaders. His tenure lasted just over two years. Still,
those years were unique to Burroughs in the fact he was the last
of the "insiders" groomed from within Burroughs to lead the
company. He was also the leader picked to follow Ray W.
Macdonald, a man who had made a great imprint on Burroughs
and was certainly a hard "act" for anyone to follow.

Although it turned out that Mr. Mirabito's management and
control would not be very long, it was momentous in the
Burroughs lifetime because he was the one who changed the
Burroughs leadership search from promoting from inside to
making the search purposely go outside.

That decision alone made his leadership a pivotal time for the
Burroughs Corporation.

He turned out to be the Burroughs leader who, along with his
Board, decided on and implemented a major shift in the way
Burroughs and its management had been heading for years. For a

variety of reasons apparent to him and his Board in 1979, the company was going to have to change to survive a brighter future.

Business Environment

In the late 70's, computer companies and their products were becoming more and more reliable and sophisticated. Support needs to run them were also changing to reflect the new quality and reliability. Computers ran much better at that time due to manufacturing and design quality. Technical support for the computers was migrating away from less and less performance interruption duties to broader company purposes and needs.

Mainframes were still the big sellers and were still being used as central information systems repositories for government and business installations.

Burroughs was very much a major player in the computer business under Mr. Mirabito but forces of competition, dwindling numbers of mainframe users to go around, and Burroughs own desire for a more robust bottom line became front and center issues.

Mr. Mirabito presided over Burroughs during the President Jimmy Carter years. This coincidentally was the time future Burroughs head, W. Michael Blumenthal, was serving as first Secretary of the Treasury to President Carter. The early ending of that government position freed Mr. Blumenthal up for new employment opportunities. Mr.Mirabito had an idea for that availability as part of his view of the future of Burroughs.

Burroughs Environment

There were two defining issues evident when Mr. Mirabito took over Burroughs management.

One was an internal situation that focused on structural issues within the organization. Mr. Macdonald's style of management was described and regarded as "centralized" and "authoritarian" by many in the media. Many companies had that style of management but the ideas for more distributed management were surfacing out in the business world too.

The other defining issue was external to Burroughs. It was about the desired position of the now mature company in the current computer marketplace. Questions about the next direction were surfacing in the company. Computer manufacturers were constantly faced with competition and changing market place requirements.

A media report of the period focused on some other Burroughs considerations:

"In one way, Burroughs is a paradox. It pays the lowest salaries in the industry…yet it has one of the best records of employee loyalty. It's a good family environment", a VP of another major company said.

"This old-fashioned paternalistic approach has paid off. For last ten years, Burroughs has averaged a 15% compounded growth in revenues and a 20% annual increase in projects (1969-1979)."

And, "Much of Burroughs success has been due to strong corporate dedication to profits.

A void in company's executive ranks (is) forcing Mirabito to go outside for a new CEO."

And, lastly, "Mirabito…has quiet, decisive style..(as opposed to) volatile Macdonald."[76]

Mirabito's Style and Goals

During the MIrabito tenure, the media reported a significant Burroughs "style" comment in 1979: "Difficulties (at Burroughs)...a shortage of senior management talent, because new managers weren't groomed during the years of Macdonald's dictatorial rule."[77]

It was Paul Mirabito who championed the idea of a move to an "outsider" management search for the first time in Burroughs' history. He put a media "voice" to ideas being considered in his Board.

Mirabito's Problem-Solving Approach

Internal: Structural Fixes

- More internal decentralization
- Less authority only at the top industry

External: Marketing Problem Fixes

- Look outside of Burroughs for fresh leadership and ideas
- Perhaps establish broader links to government and the finance

Products – Hardware

During Mr. Mirabito's reign Burroughs was producing a very complete and mature product line. Burroughs had products available all across the computer spectrum. One example of continuing new offerings was the B5900. This machine followed the successful and broad 800 Series line with further improvements to them.

Products-Software

Software products were also continually being produced for new and better ways to improve customer use and control of their installations. An example of software designed to measure and modify system performance was the SPARK (System Performance Analysis and Review Kit) package. This resource managing system allowed users to operate their systems closely and to most effectively manage their machine resources in real-time as needs dictated.

Mirabito's Legacies

Business Week published one view of Mr. Mirabito's legacies:

"Paul S. Mirabito, who will retire in 1980 after three years as chairman…could be remembered as the low-key, interim chief executive who filled a gap between two highly visible, dynamic leaders – the tough, domineering Ray W. Macdonald, who turned the reins over to him in 1978, and the aggressive W. Michael Blumenthal.

It is Mirabito who is setting the stage for Blumenthal to transform a computer maker of the 1970's into an information company of the1980's.

Burroughs has shown steady, if unexciting, growth… But, if the new team is to succeed, it will have to flush new life through Burroughs' stodgy, inbred management…new managers were not groomed during the years of Macdonald's dictatorial rule."[78]

The Die Is Cast

With the selection of W. Michael Blumenthal, the Burroughs leadership passed to a new and different style of leadership and a radically changed Burroughs.

Mr. Mirabito retired from Burroughs in 1980.

The Mirabito Era

Chapter **8**

The Mirabito Era (1977-1979)

Life Inside Burroughs - A Burroughs Branch – Lansing, Michigan
(1977-1979)

The branch at Lansing, Michigan, was one of the most active and
productive branches in the Burroughs customer field. It
developed and maintained that status in Michigan's capital area
because of some of the tightly run and very wide-spread branch
sales work done there. Granted, Lansing was the center of the
Michigan state government and Burroughs was a Michigan
corporation. But, large government information system contracts
in the 70's were very competitive and required a large amount of
up-front work, including serious benchmarking, to assure the
machines could do the job the contracts required. It was tough,
detailed work and this branch did it well.

   The Burroughs Lansing Branch was structured in the typical
Burroughs organizational style. There was a Branch Manager
with a Sales Staff, a Branch Field Engineering Manager and Field
Engineering technicians, and a Branch Systems Manager with
System Support Representatives.

Because of all the prior extensive marketing done by this branch, the branch served a heavy mix of state government and banking sites as well as hospitals, manufacturing companies, and other businesses. It was in the aggressive marketing and competition for the state's several large computer installations that the Burroughs branch sales force made such dramatic inroads as one single branch and provided such a rich array of large installations of Burroughs equipment.

Much of the early and complete foundation sales work had been done in Lansing during the Macdonald Era, as was often true in many of the branches Mr. Mirabito inherited, so the Lansing Branch by 1976 was a mature branch with mature and sophisticated customer/users.

Branches such as this did continue to do further major sales activity but also had the additional goal of upgrading and broadening their considerable existing customer installations

A-NOTE

I joined the Lansing Branch as Branch Systems Manager in 1976.

By 1976, the Burroughs Lansing Branch had many major large computer systems installed and running in such government areas as: the Michigan State Police, Treasury Department, Secretary of State, and Highway Department.

Michigan National Bank was a large financial customer in Lansing as was Sparrow Hospital in the medical area and Wolverine Shoes in the commercial area in Grand Rapids. And, there were many more.

The Burroughs available solutions to large transaction handling and the company experience in very large database storage issues were part of the success of these choices. Banking and government installations contained huge amounts of stored internal data and had the needs to access that data and preserve its integrity.

These special data-handling needs produced a serious synergistic technical growth to result between the customer's technical staffs and the Burroughs support team. And, out of this specialization, several Burroughs and customer technical staff members accomplished some pace-setting work in the world of high-volume, fast transaction data- base storage and high through-put data-communications solutions.

In a branch like this, with installations doing large and innovative technical advances with the equipment, many customers were creating real-time experiences with the computer designs in a taxing working environment. Technical activity and the resulting accomplishments were high.

The Lansing Branch

One example of innovative work being done in Lansing by customers was the implementation in 1969 of the Michigan State Police LEIN System built on a B5500 mainframe.

LEIN stood for: Law Enforcement Information Network

As noted in *DATAMATION*, the LEIN Systems was a 145 terminal data-based system for use as a real-time information resource across the state police system.[79] Coincidentally in Lansing, the Department of State auto and boat licensing information was also on Burroughs equipment. This mass information also resided in very large data-base storage areas.

Rich technical activity like these big storage needs came into play often when the need came up for bidding for contracts for new systems and when benchmarks were needed to be held to insure a site and Burroughs could make the contracted goals. Abundant technical information delivery and informational support also was needed with each major software release Burroughs provided for the customers through-out the branch area.

And this branch, as was the case with many other branches, sometimes required special technical assistance provided by Burroughs Corporation as a whole when a customer had a pressing issue at hand that was specific to one special technical area of the customer's installation.

B-NOTE

The Lansing Branch by its very nature became a productive source of support technical leadership for:

1. **Large and Very Large Systems installations**
2. **Customer use of very large and critical data bases and their reliability**
3. **Customer use of very high and critical transaction rates and data communications reliability.**
4. **Technical expertise in benchmarking specialized large systems up-time requirements such as data-bases and transaction communications.**

A-NOTE

An instance of this specialized assistance came up at one of the large sites in Lansing involving how to improve and utilize their large database systems.

One of the excellent Burroughs company-wide data-base specialists was contacted and he provided on-site assistance in this area for them.

The interesting situation for me as a Branch Systems Manager at the status meeting called to discuss the

specialist's evaluation results was to see how the analyzed suggestions would be accepted by the site's technical team. By concept, some of the government sites are "military" in structure and some are more "laid-back". This site was more of the military type.

Those of us on the Burroughs technical team, and particularly the sales representatives, were more than aware that each customer is different in how they react to information and how they prefer to have it communicated to them. Quality support was best tuned to the needs of the customer as part of doing business.

The result of this particular meeting was fascinating to me. The Burroughs technical specialist who knew what he was talking about gave it all straight out concerning what he thought and what they ought to do. As many good technical minds will do, he pulled no punches. The customer site information team had asked for help and they therefore took the analysis and recommendations in totally good faith. He gave it, they were very pleased, and our sales representative relaxed.

The value of "telling-it-like-it-is" in business, like in most other enterprises, usually turned out to be the best direction and the only way to go. Many, many status meetings that approached the difficult subjects

in that way more effectively solved problems.

Significantly in the Lansing area, most of the customers employed very savvy technical staff and Burroughs correspondingly made every effort to supply support to their needs with equally professionally energized personnel.

Corporate Home Office Link

During the Mirabito years, the Lansing Branch activities were certainly directed, evaluated, and motivated from the Mirabito Corporate Home Office. The steady release of new and better product solutions seemed to keep coming along sufficiently to keep Burroughs very prominent in the game and offer continuing advancements for its customers.

So, in general, business appeared to be going along relatively well and calm, much as Mr. Mirabito was himself during his interim leadership at the helm of Burroughs.

As in many companies facing major internal issues, the big changes and shake-ups soon to come within Burroughs were still mostly home office issues and considerations and were not on the field priority lists yet.

A-NOTE

I transferred to the Detroit Technical Support Organization (MSC-Detroit)) in 1978 just as Mr.

Mirabito's leadership time was ending. I was going back into to the home office environment (with all that means) as W. Michael Blumenthal came on the scene.

To return to the corporate home environment at this time in Burroughs history turned out be an exciting and fortuitous move. The Blumenthal era was beginning.

As an unexpected bonus, my Lansing Branch experiences and the robust technical environment there were coming with me back to the Burroughs home office area with an increased respect for what the Burroughs Corporation and its customers could achieve together.

Chapter 9

The W. Michael Blumenthal Era (1979-1986)

The Last of the Five Final Leaders

W. Michael Blumenthal was the fifth and last CEO of Burroughs' final 40 years.

His management was significant in so many ways, including bringing Burroughs into a merger with Sperry Corporation.

He brought to Burroughs his career in business, government, and economics as someone outside of Burroughs. His resume included having been an economist, in charge of the Bendix Corporation, and having been the first Secretary of the Treasury under President Jimmy Carter.

From The New York Times News Service: "W. Michael Blumenthal, a former Princeton University Economics professor... stayed 2 ½ years with the Carter Administration...was CEO of Bendix four years."[80]

His style, background, and being someone not in the computer business were unique qualities that were apparently sought by Paul Mirabito and the Burroughs Board when they picked W. Michael Blumenthal. As quoted in *Electronic News*, "The choice of Mr. Blumenthal was mine," Paul S. Mirabito.[81]

The Blumenthal Era

In 1979, *Business Week* stated: "(re: Burroughs problems)…Mirabito – has spent much of the last 20 months grappling with the management shortcomings that created them."[82]

Newsweek noted about WMB (Blumenthal), "…an economist….no experience in the computer business…a general management background."[83]

Paul Mirabito said, "…he's (WMB) well acquainted in the financial marketplace."[84]

Mr. Blumenthal presided over Burroughs for seven years before the 1986 merger, and those years were possibly the most highly-active and volatile years in the Burroughs story. Mr. Blumenthal was different in style from his predecessors at Burroughs, representing change in all the sense of that word for Burroughs, and would forge the new manner and way Burroughs proceeded into the 80's.

Ironically, in 1985, the Burroughs Corporation as a company achieved its 100th anniversary in American business history. The name was gone one year later.

The Choice of an "Outsider"

The coming of the W. Michael Blumenthal era to Burroughs opened an extremely important and course-changing point in the company's history in many ways.

First, it was a landmark decision by the Board of Directors to pick a chairman not of the computer industry nor an in-house rising performer.

As noted earlier, W. Michael Blumenthal was an economist, had previous corporate experience at Bendix Corp, and was Secretary of Treasury under President Carter but was not a "computer" man as such. He did bring experience and connections in government that could be very important to Burroughs, which marketed to the defense industry as part of its Line-of-Business plan.

As a back-story, the story of Bendix and Blumenthal's part in that story was an interesting prelude to his assignment at Burroughs. His style appeared to be very different from his predecessors Ray MacDonald and Paul Mirabito at Burroughs but the direction Burroughs wanted appeared to be in a strong drive to be much more than one of the seven dwarfs of computing and instead make a major run at IBM. These were continuing to be very competitive times for the computing industry and there were casualties all along the way still occurring among the small strugglers.

A prophetic article in *Business Week* reported: "Analysts feel that Blumenthal will have to lead Burroughs into new businesses, perhaps by acquisition, in the 1980's to continue the company's growth."[85]

As to Blumenthal's style at previous employer Bendix, the *Business Journal* noted: "Blumenthal's record…at Bendix…shows that he chooses his subordinates carefully, and lets them run their own business. He stays out of the day-to-day operations and delegates that responsibility further down the management ranks..."[86]

Blumenthal Early Changes

As the *Wall Street Journal* saw Burroughs in 1981:"...Burroughs changes in troubled operations: ... leave insiders, most top managers, unlike earlier outsiders (did)... more decisions at lower levels of management...not (like) past centralized...quicker and better decisions...open channels of communications.

New: Corporate Project Management Activity headed by Wm. P Conlon, VP Sales, specialize in Banking, Finance, Health Care, Education"[87]

The Expectations

In 1980, the *Florida Times Union* printed a piece on Mr. Blumenthal and Burroughs commenting on them both.

"Burroughs has recently run into stormy financial weather...

...Burroughs reputation in some quarters for being tight-fisted with employees, less than forth-right with security analysts and slow to act on customer's complaints...

Critics also fault it for a narrow product line and insular management.

The Burroughs Corporation

One of Blumenthal's main challenges will be to loosen the grip held by Ray Macdonald, who in a decade as chief executive beginning in 1967, personally transformed Burroughs from an enterprise synonymous with the adding machine into a major computer company.

But, Macdonald was so loathe to delegate responsibility that he was also in effect the head of the public relations and personnel departments as well as chief product planner and head of the complaint department.

…(there is a) paucity of new products and a shortage of semiconductors, which analysts say are indicative Burroughs has not been keeping up with technology.

(WMB)…it is true that we do have some problems."

And, "Blumenthal…faces a number of hurdles if he is to pull Burroughs out of the doldrums." [88]

The *Detroit Free Press* observed in 1980, "---for WMB, two areas (are) crucial. One is strategic planning. The other is software – the programming software and services are 1/3 of cost of a systems package…soon to be 1/2 or more."[89]

Noted in "Ticker Talk", "(re) BGH (Burroughs) stock…W. Michael Blumenthal, selection of chief executive officer, policy changes and stratagems this company sorely needs."[90]

B-NOTE

At the CUBE convention in Anaheim, California, in 1979, W. Michael Blumenthal addressed the customer-user group for the first time in his role as new chief operating officer of Burroughs. He appeared prominently at the opening session as featured speaker and for the first time for many, outlined his vision for the corporation. This was a special address for several reasons. He was the first non-Burroughs computer-experienced chief operating officer recently elected to the position and he was bringing his unique style in from service at The Bendix Corporation and as former Secretary of the Treasury under President Carter.

A-NOTE

As part of my assigned duties in large systems support at MSC-Detroit, I was at the Anaheim CUBE assisting Mr. Tom Grier, CUBE management liaison for Burroughs.

I, like so many others, was eager to hear the Blumenthal speech so was able to be in the audience at that landmark opening session. Many Burroughs company people were in the audience along with the customers.

Two interesting side-points impressed me about that Blumenthal speech in addition to finding it a very important and a well-delivered speech to hear. Mr.

Blumenthal was there on the stage and at the dais dressed in muted browns…a rather stark difference from the mostly dark blue and black suits popular in corporate circles of the day. That set a certain tone, I thought, and also made it very easy to pick him out.

The other point was the fact he noticeably spoke without benefit of a written speech. He had what looked like some small 3 by 5 cards in his hands but he gave the speech structured mainly in his mind and linked his thoughts completely and effectively. Motivational and vision speeches given in that way seem to hit their mark effectively and it was pretty certain Mr. Blumenthal wanted to deliver a "convincer" that day both to the customers and to the company.

What Was Going On In America

1. The decade of the 80's had begun.
2. President Ronald Reagan was in the White House.
3. Corporate mergers and takeovers were popular and on the rise.
4. This was to be the decade of the rise of the Personal Computer.
5. The large centralized mainframe computers were

becoming a smaller market for the computing business.

The Blumenthal Era

Government Business Environment 1980

Noted in the *Buckeye Business Journal*: ""Executives agreed nearly unanimously in the likelihood of some specific measures the Reagan administration would propose to stimulate productivity – tax breaks…and an easing of regulatory burdens on business. Few executives expect a ready end to excessively high inflation. "No one solution will work," says W.M. Blumenthal…we expect double-digit inflation to persist through 1981.""[91]

Blumenthal's Early Approaches

1980 Earnings

"Burroughs says it is consolidating plants, phasing out some production lines and changing accounting procedures. The move comes in the wake of Burroughs 1st quarterly earnings decline in 17 years (1963)."[92] Those 17 years included the management of both Ray Macdonald and Paul Mirabito.

Also, from the *Syracuse Herald Journal*: "W. Michael Blumenthal blamed declines (in earnings) on: previously announced difficulties in bringing a large number of new products on stream and out of the plants as quickly as planned.

Burroughs discontinued its Burroughs Scientific Processor operations. Other actions: phasing out calculator and adding machine products, closing some small overseas subsidiary operations and changing inventory valuations, including provisions for obsolescence."[93]

The Burroughs Corporation

Blumenthal economic thoughts were noted in 1981 in the *Farmington Observer* that in recent previous years, "...national & economic woes – low rates of production, savings, large capital formation, virtual absence of long-term planning by private industry and government. A need: Government, Business, and Labor (together)."[94]

The *Miami Herald* noted in1981: "Burroughs Corporation has begun a "major and significant reorganization" of its top management that will end the centralized management structure it had become known for", says Chairman W. Blumenthal."[95]

Also in 1981, the *Detroit Free Press* noted: "W. M. Burroughs will decentralize its management over the next 18-24 months and try to win customers by emphasizing "systems rather than boxes". (WMB) modified the titles or duties of 14 high-ranking executives and formed committees for: weakness, inability to provide timely and efficient delivery and service to customers after the sale."[96]

Things were changing rapidly in the computing field. Hardware was settling down, becoming much more reliable, and requiring much less attention. The machines ran and ran well. Modular replacement was replacing on-site debugging by field engineers. Also software also ran much better and longer. This was directing how a manufacturer placed the service personnel and implying new areas of revenue had to be developed.

The old "packaging" of software components (bundling) was moving to the practice of separate billing for software packages. That meant new, innovative software products like code-generating software had to come into the pipeline to keep ahead of the game.

And, there was that "upstart" invention, the personal or micro computer, emerging in the mainframe-focused computing industry.

One specific Burroughs approach to the inclusion of third parties in software for their products resulted in the forming of their ISO unit in 1980. "Burroughs forms ISO (Independent Sales Organization) to cement closer ties to the third party software firms writing applications programs for Burroughs equipment."[97]

Defense Business

Burroughs continued its substantial military and defense business in the Blumenthal era. The company had its Federal and Special Systems Group created specifically for that market and Burroughs also formed a new Air Force Division in that group in 1980.[98]

"The Radar System, ARTSII (Automated Radar Terminal System), ...(has been) installed at Lowell Field (Chattanooga)...(also in 69 other airports). Development by Burroughs, Paoli, PA, ...does records keeping and identification activity for controllers."[99]

And, an example for the Air Force: "$45.2 million contract, Phase IV Base Level Data Automation Program...Burroughs Federal and Special Systems Group, Paoli....104 bases"[100]

The Burroughs Corporation

The B20 and the Personal Computer Tsunami

In MSC-Detroit in 1979-1980, a strange little terminal-like piece of equipment showed up named the B20. There amidst all the on-going support for the Burroughs family of mainframe computer systems was a new Burroughs baby…a version of a PC (Personal Computer) or mini-computer.

In most ways, it looked like a normal Burroughs terminal of the time - black case, usual screen size, and keyboard. But, it was much more than that.

Business Week noted in 1979: "To succeed in the1989's, Burroughs must become a lot more aggressive in small computers. It will have to open retail stores to sell its small systems.

The company already is planning to enter the minicomputer business. It has not decided how it will enter this market but it will probably (be) either a minicomputer company or strip its small business systems of their software and peripherals and market the computer alone. From there, hints Burroughs' DuRay Stromback, it is a small step into home computers."[101]

In 1981, Blumenthal's opinion was reported in the *Detroit Free Press*: "Blumenthal said Burroughs will continue to

specialize in large computers. It will avoid the home and hobby market, he said, but is developing a "very small big system" to sell in 8K-10K range."[102]

An industry view was printed in the Philadelphia *Focus:* "Manufacturers of large computer systems such as IBM…and Burroughs are the late starters in the small computer game, playing catch-up to Apple, Radio Shack, and Commodore Business Machines. The name of the computer game is changing as the newer, smaller, and creative companies enter the small computer market."[103]

Although a novelty in many ways, this B20 made its debut very quietly amidst a huge active mainframe installation and support business going on in the industry, with Burroughs right there in the midst of it. Burroughs obviously was looking into the PC. But, their business was overwhelmingly as a mainframe supplier. In early 1984, Burroughs publicized the newer B25 computer; the B20 was bought from Convergent Technologies.

In the same citing, an analyst for Arthur D. Little & Co., Ted Withington, caught the effect of the growing personal computer: "For strategic reasons, Burroughs declines to reveal plans (for the PC). In some sense, they can't avoid them," an analyst said (Withington).

The distinction between PC and other machines are blurred. "Personal computers are merging with general purpose machines," Withington said. "---they (Burroughs) must offer multi-purpose work stations…"[104]

Later, in 1985, Barry Stavro of *FORBES* observed in the article "Room at the Top": "Large computers aren't the only reason next year (1986) looks good for Burroughs. The company is finally making some headway in small office computers…with

Convergent Technologies."[105]

Office Systems Group

Burroughs under Blumenthal didn't ignore the word-processing and small office systems market. They approached it in part by creating the Office Systems Group in 1981, marketing to the low-end word-processing customer with the RIII machine in three series: 315, 325, 335.

The Burroughs approach was towards automated office systems rather than the PC minicomputers surfacing in the industry. That approach made best use of their existing product lines. The eventual market blessing needed for that approach was another matter.

Office of the Future

As a further focus on office-oriented solutions, the *Detroit Free Press* noted in 1984 that Burroughs "…made a belated plunge into the "Office of the Future" concept".[106]

Acquisitions

From the *Detroit Free Press*: "Blumenthal's first acquisition was Systems Development Corporation (of California)…got – skilled employees in software and programming as well as electronics engineers."[107]

Burroughs also acquired Memorex and Graphics Technology Corporation of Boulder, Colorado in this era. Graphics Technology Corporation was a CAD /CAM supplier (Computer Aided Design). It became GRAFTEK, a Burroughs company.[108]

Plants

From the beginning of W. M. Blumenthal's tenure, Burroughs continued to open plants and close some others showing the vast amount of shifting and adjustment needed for rapidly changing markets.

In 1980, the *Pomona Progress Bulletin* listed these Burroughs' plants in Southern California: Mission Viejo, City of Industry, Santa Ana, Westlake Village, Carlsbad, Rancho Bernardo, San Diego, and Pasadena. [109]

In 1980, The *Clearwater Sun* reported: "Burroughs to build an engineering and manufacturing center in Orlando for advanced computer printing devices."[110]

In 1981, the media noted: "Burroughs to build a plant (Georgetown, Texas)."[111]

And, "Burroughs may lay off 75 workers at Coral Springs, (FL)."[112]

Also, "Burroughs building a major plant in SW Jacksonville, 2/17/81."[113]

The Burroughs Corporation

On the negative side; the media noted in early 1981: "No new product manufacturing at three Detroit plants (Tireman Ave, Plymouth, Wayne)...phase out over three to four years...(due to) wages and manufacturing costs."[114]

And later in 1981, "Burroughs may close two area (Detroit) manufacturing plants...unless...change in manufacturing costs...that improves competitive costs of doing business here."
[115]

In 1981, Burroughs announced plans to move some manufacturing from their Wayne, Michigan plant to their Plymouth plant, specifically their S3000 series sorters.[116]

Announced in 1985: "Closed plants – Piscataway, Plainfield, and Croydon, England; B25 to be built at Raritan (NJ) plant."[117]

Products - Hardware

Burroughs continued to announce an impressive array of new products under WMB's leadership:

In 1980, "Burroughs said Mission Viejo (their California Large Systems plant) is now making the new B6900 series."[118]

The smaller B1855 was coming out of the Santa Barbara plant.

Also, the *Electronic News* noted: "The new B3950 computer is on definite hold, Burroughs says...(hasn't performed at level). The new 90's are: B90, B900, B1900, B2900, B3900, B5900, B6900."[119]

The Blumenthal Era

In a 1980 associated posting, Burroughs announced the B920 small business computer for standalone and distributed processing.[120]

The announcement of the B6900 Series was followed in September 1980 by another technically advanced announcement:

"Burroughs introduces the B5930 Computer System (very modular) out of Mission Viejo."

DATAMATION noted: "The B5900, a new machine mapped closely to high level programming the B6500 introduced in 1966."[121]

Also in 1980, the company revealed: "Burroughs is expected to expand its product offering and become a full-line supplier for the "automated office of the future."[122] This was an important attempt to look in newer directions than just mainframe production.

Also in 1981, *Information System News* reported: WMB – intends to bring out the B4900 and B7900 in 1981."[123]

Later hardware products coming out of Burroughs displayed a new, changed nomenclature for two new series of computers that broke free of the familiar "BXXX" nomenclature scheme. These new series were called the "A" Series and "V" Series.

The "A" Series

The Burroughs Corporation

First to be announced in the newly renamed machine series was the "A" series, followed by the "V "series. The "A" series were large systems and the "V" series were medium systems.

In March, 1985: the *Wall Street Journal* reported: "A15 arrived."[124] The A3, the second member of the "A" Series, was announced on 2/85 by Burroughs.[125] Noted in 1984, "The A9 has increased IBM communications capabilities."[126] In late 1985, "The A10F (1-processor) and A10H (2-processor) were announced."[127]

By 1986, the "A" Series contained machines including the A3, A5, A9.A10, A12, and A15.

The emergence of the Burroughs newer wide-ranging A Series hitting the market offered by Burroughs was purposely compatible with older Burroughs equipment so that a user could migrate relatively easily to the A Series platforms.

The "V" Series

The "V" series medium systems replacement scheme was noted in *COMPUTERWORLD* in April 1985: "Burroughs announced the V340 and V380 replacing the B4925 and B4955".[128]

Reader-Sorters

Burroughs also continued making a broad line of other products that were important to the corporate bottom-line.

An example was the B9190 MICR/OCR document processor (checks) announced in early 1981.

Products – Software

In the critical area of the customer's need for computers to communicate with each other, Burroughs announced a software product called BNA (Burroughs Network Architecture),

B-NOTE

Burroughs Key (No. 18) Designed for portability of products across machine lines

Code Generating Software

Offerings of code generating software were finding their niche in computer user sites as a simple tool for creating programs automatically using data definitions and the automatic generating of running code.

Burroughs offered code-generating software that allowed the users to design and build their own database and database accessing programs.

For any user installation, the ability to create code and make their own unique accessing programs was a major cost-cutting boon to the old cost of maintaining on-site programmers.

Burroughs had a product for this need called LINC II.

LINC II (Logic and Information Network Compiler II)

LINC II was a Burroughs system introduced in 1982 that would generate running program code in various languages for the user. "It was a fourth generation application systems generator. The software was developed by Gil Spencer and Peter Harkin of New Zealand. This information systems generator included: a common database, definitions that encode, and generates views of data for business information."[129]

This was a major step by Burroughs to give the user the ability to generate code for its site that had documentation included to show how the programs were built. That assistance and ability directly compared favorably with the costly wide-spread use of on-site programmers and the need to continually support these home-grown programs over the years.

Open Systems Interconnection (OSI)

As noted in *Data Communications* in 1983, Burroughs was looking into the OSI (Open Systems Interconnection) protocol as part of its goal, along with many others in the market, to find new ways to link dissimilar machines. "OSI…is a down-to-earth answer to networking computers and terminals of all types and manufacturers.[130]

Continuity of Vendor Support

The important promise from manufacturers that new software releases and hardware systems would be continually supported was now a prominent factor for users to think about. Support translates to budgeting money for manufacturers and having enough resources to support older and out of date systems. This issue was on the table for possible cost-containment in the industry. Announcements were coming out stating there would be support cut-offs ahead.

It was to a user's advantage to keep on current releases and not to fall too behind on systems design so support would be there.

On the technical support side for Burroughs, the systems were proving to be more reliable and much more durable over the years. Both manufacturer and users could see it without doubt. Components and modular packaging were saving energy and heat and were delivering longer productive life.

Hardware was becoming so reliable, attention needs by Burroughs field engineers were changing. This trend had a major effect on staffing decisions and personnel use as well as cost considerations in total customer installation support requirements. A similar change was occurring on the systems software support side.

A-NOTE

The machine at the Burroughs site (community

college) where I was employed in 1984 was a B6800 and was a working example of the value of the benefits of migrating to a new platform. We migrated with Burroughs to an A5 as part of the above mentioned assurance of continuing current support needs and having access to updated features. The migration was easy and done without incident and we were then current, where we wanted to be.

What The Media Was Saying

In 1981, a local Detroit area paper said, "W. Michael Blumenthal...warns of slow economic recovery. (Only) two plants left in Detroit area - Wayne and Plymouth. (Nation has)...economic woes: low rates of production, savings, large capital formation. ...Virtual absence of long-term planning by private industry and government. Need: (to solve:)...Government, Business, and Labor."[131]

A-NOTE

In 2009, the old "saw" about history repeating itself fits amazingly well to note Mr. Blumenthal's advice in 1981 could be printed and apply today. Business case studies can and do have a message. Mr. Marchione (then of Fiat Motors) is profiled in an article in *Time* magazine (June, 2009) dealing with how to revive the Chrysler Corporation through: promoting young

blood from below in the ranks, by-passing some older upper level managers, reorganizing Chrysler, and restructuring with a new plan. All of these same issues were in play in 1979 at Burroughs when Mr. Blumenthal took over, leaving with us the added information of how that situation worked out.

Burroughs Speaks Up

Always the quiet company, Burroughs significantly changed its advertising stripes in 1984 as noted in *Computer & Electronics Marketing*:

"Arthur Selkowitz, president, Penchina, says that for years Burroughs has been handicapped by another image problem, that of "The Big Silent Company" because it never advertised."[132]

In 1979, *Business Week* earlier noted:" Burroughs nick-named the secret computer company by industry."[133]

Mr. Blumenthal was about to change all that.

"Once the new line (new small computers) is announced, Burroughs will use: corporate and specific product campaigns…visible on all media fronts, network TV, magazine advertising, newspaper ads and radio spots...

The emphasis on advertising…is a significant reflection on the change and priorities since Mike Blumenthal took over as chair of Burroughs. A $10 million ad campaign."[134]

Blumenthal's Later Approach

In the Burroughs Corporate Communications Collection First Quarter News Highlights (1984) the article "Burroughs looks like a Contender again" stated: "Burroughs image is refurbished, the results of a renewed emphasis on quality, service, and professionalism. 1983 recorded a new high in revenue and rising profits – plowing a record $260 million into R & D of new products."[135]

In 1985, WMB's on-going ideas were documented in *DATALINK*: "Blumenthal developed two strategies – the line of business spread, where we (Burroughs) would focus our activity by market sector, and, secondly, because we had not structured our support in the way the market required, the Systems Services business was started."[136]

And, also in 1985: "Blumenthal enlarges company's sales force by 15% this year

(1985)…jacked up sales training budget to $67 million.

To blast out of the BUNCH, Burroughs will have to double in size in the next five years, Blumenthal says. (BUNCH: Burroughs, Univac, NCR, Control Data, Honeywell).

An acquisition would boost growth quickly. But, Sperry rebuffed Burroughs' bid earlier this year. Blumenthal continues to hunt for merger candidates."[137]

The Blumenthal Era

Blumenthal's Image and Style

Five Blumenthal approaches eventually surfaced as focuses of interest:

Utilize the Line-of-Business marketing approach

Bring business friends and former associates into the organization

Decentralize management

Utilize Focus Groups

Restructure systems support to the customers

Burroughs Highs and Lows

Unfortunately in business life, "lows" can pop up as well as soaring "highs".

The Quality Books law-suit was one such instance.

"Quality Books, Incorporated, of Northbrook, Illinois, a book distributor and publishing firm sued Burroughs $1.85 million on three counts of fraud and misrepresentation.

(Quality Books was a Burroughs B800 customer).

Quality ran an ad in the Wall Street Journal to find other users having problems - 400 responses.

Burroughs counter-sued, saying ads were malicious. $1.8 million in damages and two Quality officers be enjoined from speaking to news media or potential customers."[138]

Burroughs Approaching the Merger

By 1985, and then into 1986, the idea of a possible merger between Burroughs and some company became more and more fact than just a fiction. Such a major possibility had its effect, both within and outside Burroughs.

Because of the merger possibility, there were accompanying rumors and uncertainties beginning to surface.

Also, several information business factors were converging by the mid-1980's:

> Provide customer support more remotely and in more centralized centers to maximize effectiveness.

> Technical support centers were being an industry trend was emerging to restructured and support personnel faced unexpected moves and relocations to fit these rapidly changing needs.

> The real future or fate of the PC and Burroughs was looming to be resolved.

> The persisting emergence of the need to provide and support the newer networking nodes concepts versus continuing mainframe configuration support was yet

another major challenge descending on vendors and their customers.

And, the mass movement from and slowing effect of a shrinking mainframe market plus rapidly changing

theories on how to support current information systems was now important.

The question for Burroughs was: How exactly would W. M. Blumenthal and his Board define the future of Burroughs, prepare for that new definition, and what steps would Burroughs take to achieve it?

Chapter 10

The Blumenthal Era (1979-1986)

Life Inside Burroughs - The Systems Support Center (MSC-Detroit) (1978-1981)

By 1979, the central technical support activities in Detroit had changed significantly from the very active early full-line support days of the original STS (Sales Technical Services) in the late 60's and early '70's. Technical support for the multi-machine three major series of computer systems was now becoming more centered at separate newly evolving sites around the country and these location changes were making a difference in what support activities remained and were featured by Burroughs in Detroit.

For instance, Large Systems Support once so heavily centered in Detroit was now migrating to locations at Paoli, Pennsylvania, and out to California at the Mission Viejo plant. Medium Systems Support was becoming centralized in Atlanta, Georgia. These changes were being made for presumably cost and performance reasons; however, the changes were forcing changes in staff career decisions for employees back in Detroit as well.

There were still personnel representing all the computer series in the Detroit area but the now-named MSC-Detroit group evolved into taking on different and broader technical support assignments than in the past. The group did more than just machine and operating system support now.

Significant among those new assignments was an MSC-Detroit offering to do site system audits for a client to check overall performance of their information system department and evaluate their use of the equipment for a fee. MSC also conducted internal classes for Burroughs staff on how to do a site audit. Doing a good site audit required personnel with a strong customer installation experience base. MSC-Detroit attracted such talent to it.

Another function represented in MSC-Detroit was support for presenting major system or equipment releases to the customer field and Burroughs staffs. New software and hardware releases necessitated having information and supporting materials ready and in place to support the new designs. Major design implementations required having a training plan for Burroughs systems people out in the branches as well as the interested customer personnel. Preparing these release training plans was done by assembling a group of Burroughs specialists to go to the production plant involved and prepare a release training package to be used all across Burroughs. Selected personnel came from all over Burroughs including some from the MSC-Detroit staff.

B-NOTE

The Burroughs Corporation

Burroughs Key (No. 19) Invest in training for both staff and customers

Also located in MSC-Detroit was technical support for the customer user group CUBE (Cooperating Users of Burroughs Equipment), which was the bi-annual user group convention held at different major American cities each year. The Burroughs part of the management of CUBE was done in the Detroit World Headquarters with planning underway year round for each conference event.

The B5900 Computer System Introduction Survey

MSC-Detroit also was one source turned to for technical personnel to do specialized marketing requests such as conducting a survey of early users of the B5900 computer system introduction to determine how the new machines were being accepted and installed.

Being a support group located in the very shadow of the World Headquarters gave MSC-Detroit and its technical personnel some special assignments that were needed by Marketing or similar group.

In the B5900 introduction case, feed-back from first installations indicated there might be some problems with the installation going in successfully.

This information generated a need for Burroughs to find out how the introduction of the newly released B5900 computer system was being received by the customers in 1980. Information coming back to the corporation via on-site technical personnel, local sales staff, and resulting branch and district feedback hinted their might be some timing and problem response issues to iron out and that's when Burroughs responded with a plan.

It sent out a technical staff person to go on-site to four newly purchased B5900 computer systems customers and have a good old-fashioned sit-down talk with the customers on how things were going for them.

The four sites chosen were in the Mid-West Region served out of Detroit.

The survey was intended to be not so much formal as to be a chance for good listening and hopefully resulting in learning something to improve the future installations as well as those surveyed.

A-NOTE

During the first installations of the B5900's, as mentioned above, Burroughs was receiving word from the early sites that there were some issues arising about installation problems.

To find out what the issues were, I was the survey person assigned to this study from MSC-Detroit. Burroughs often sent trouble-shooters and specialists to customer sites that need attention...as part of how Burroughs operated and responded with special support where it was needed. This survey assignment was called for because early information was sketchy or missing. Going on-site was deemed to be the best way to do some good.

The project required flying to four sites and meeting with the customers. It was a fascinating project and resulted in some very satisfying fact-finding. As a result, new installation procedures and changes were created by Burroughs, specifically the need and advisability to stage the assembly of full computer systems prior to shipment to customers so there would be no unnecessary complications or delays installing the machine at the customer site.

The idea was to wring out set-up problems before the machine arrived at the customer's site. This pre-setup avoided delays and parts surprises and speeded up the installation process. Any problems could be resolved before the hardware actually reached the customer site. Valuable operations delay time was avoided.

B-NOTE

In response to this customer input and information,, in 1981, Burroughs announced they had implemented: "Six Staging Centers – USA, to integrate and test equipment before shipping. Detroit was one center."[139]

Other MSC-Detroit Mandates

The need continued for support for specialized software offerings such as data-communications, database management, performance measurement, and other support needs at the time to be available, especially with the World Headquarters nearby to generate original requests at any time.

In this time period of Burroughs history, the company was pursuing the use of interactive software producing systems (LINC II) in addition to their already successful GEMCOS data communications program generation. Also, a popular performance measuring tool was (SPARK), which allowed a technician to create a specifically tuned analysis of a system.

MSC-Detroit was able to provide support for software systems like these if needed.

Customer Site Audits

As a manufacturer of information systems, Burroughs was often asked for advice by customers on how to most efficiently run their equipment. This need was met by the MSC-Detroit Site Audit program, which was staffed with technical specialists best suited to evaluate a customer. The outcome was usually a report and formal presentation based on an on-site visit. Audits such as this were coming out of MSC-Detroit in the 1979-1981 time period.

B-NOTE

The experiences of Burroughs technical people at former sites and former jobs gave valuable insight on how different users ran their businesses and how problems can arise that can be foreseen and prevented as well.

Those experiences and further knowledge gained through doing on-site audits allowed Burroughs personnel to create materials for doing site-auditing and to pass on outlines on how to do that service to other Burroughs technical staff via training classes.

A-NOTE

Two specific audits I was involved with during my MSC-Detroit time were an audit for an insurance company and an International site audit at a federal

department site of the Mexican government in Mexico City.

Both were interesting studies for our team to address. Both were hopefully of help to the clients and the teams were able to come up with very specific suggestions based on pre-planned questions MSC-Detroit had developed to guide the audits.

Being in the international setting of Mexico City for an audit was icing on the cake for those of us on the three-man Burroughs team sent there. Our hosts were most gracious to us and the audit was a learning situation for all of us even above and beyond the technical aspects.

A-NOTE

Often, on-site audits revealed long-ignored local issues simply by the fact someone who understands shows up and listens well. An audit can be a very simple way to open up important blocked avenues of communication at the audit site.

We found site problems and issues often held the best answers already within the site. The need was to let them surface successfully.

The Burroughs Corporation

Software and Hardware Releases

An important major function of Burroughs central technical support groups was the repeating task of moving a new software release out to the customer base. Software was constantly undergoing improvement by the production of fixes (or "patches") for specific problems and issues. But, all the manufacturers had the task of putting all the fixes and new features eventually into a major level release for their customers.

These releases were usually tapes and documentation accompanied by some method of training for both Burroughs personnel and customer staff.

In that spirit, releases were targeted for each system design series in the three-tier Burroughs machine stable.

The B6800 Global Memory System

At the end of the 70's, the Burroughs Large Systems group offered the new B6800 Global Memory system which was a multiple processor design capable of running as a single multi-processor system or splitting itself into separate processors with different forms of memory allocation possibilities. The concept was very innovative and gave a user much more flexibility in how to use a machine in distinctly different ways and configurations over a 24-hour period.

To bring this innovative design to market, an MSC-Detroit member was part of the team sent to the Mission Viejo California plant to prepare the release.

B-NOTE

Burroughs was truly showing its research and advanced design expertise with the B6800 Global Memory System. This technical design was a mark of their trying to make products more versatile and more usable for the users through the ability to change the machine's reconfiguration at will.

We on the selected release team received the support information at the plant and found the system worked as advertised when plant personnel gave us a demo at the end of the in-plant training. The concept was technical enough and versatile enough to challenge innovative ways of providing information for it. The initial team represented technical specialists from all over the Burroughs support system plus training from the plant designers, who were very casual California personnel compared to us used to serving on the more formal Mid-West customer front.

The plant designers had put the concept of "Casual Friday" in effect all week long then well before the more relaxed style of the coming Silicon Valley period

became normal in business. We were in suits and business apparel; they were in sandals and polo shirts and shorts.

But, the necessary information transfer came off very well.

A-NOTE

The methods for training at that time were basically lecture, overheads, and handouts. That mix required the would-be trainers to do some intense digging and questioning to be able to answer eventual questions in the future release classrooms. A lot of reading and a lot of dialog were necessary but the payoff for each training employee was the deeper knowledge of how this unique information system worked.

They then prepared the appropriate training materials used to spread essential information throughout the company and customer base.

The CUBE User Information Exchange Conventions

One customer communication enterprise Burroughs thought very highly of and supported enthusiastically was the user group CUBE (Cooperating Users of Burroughs Equipment).

This group provided important avenues for information exchange between users and the corporation as well as to insure this vital communication link was addressed formally at least twice a year at the bi-annual conventions. The CUBE schedule featured a convention location plan that had attendees going to an eastern city in the fall and a western city in the spring.

In the setting of a week-long convention held usually in a very attractive American city, Burroughs could release new technical information to key users and the same users could voice reactions and experiences with Burroughs via panel discussions and user talks about the products.

There was also a similar user organization operating in the Burroughs international customer base.

Although the CUBE users' group belonged to the users, Burroughs provided a coordinating officer in Detroit and facilities for managing the logistics for the group all year long.

This coordinating position was being run in the late 70's and early 80's by Mr. Tom Grier at the Burroughs World Headquarters.   And, to assist Mr. Grier, MSC-Detroit provided some technical support for him at the conventions.

A-NOTE

Since many of the CUBE convention sessions were by intent very technical and required the presence of

designers and programmers to be there from the development centers, CUBE was always an interesting mix of personality types meeting together to present and learn from each other. The mix had customers, managers, and staff integrated with Burroughs Sales and Technical Representatives. CUBE was created as a user group and was not a sales area as such. Burroughs sales people were there to represent Burroughs but mainly to be available as assistance to the users.

One of the more volatile outcomes and fascinating interplays in meetings and sessions would be the often very "straight shooting" and "off-the-cuff" comments and thoughts offered by the normally very isolated software and hardware designers and therefore some very interesting revelations of their thought processes not usually featured in a normal sales sessions. Many of the customers loved the candor, however.

And, as all business sales people know, there were also the carefully prepared demonstrations that wouldn't work when required.

But, there were extremely important exchanges at these meetings, in sessions, at coffee breaks, and at dinner out on the host town. Features and changes would show up at the next CUBE because of those opportunities.

MSC-Detroit

Burroughs customer loyalty was always an important part of how the corporation remained viable for 101 years in the face of intense competition. It is a business asset Burroughs did have and so nurtured it.

Both CUBE and the efforts of such departments as MSC-Detroit were focused on maintaining that loyalty relationship. That focus also rebounded in a secondary way positively within the Burroughs "family" at the time. In the next years to follow, as massive changes and the volatile times arrived at most corporations, the Burroughs "family" loyalty was to be severely challenged.

Chapter 11

The Blumenthal Era (1979-1986)

Life Outside Burroughs – The View as a Customer (1980-1986)

A Large System User Experience

One of the most significant views of a corporation comes from the position of being a customer-user of its products and services.

Everything the company tries to be and do ends up appearing in some form at the customer's site.

Especially important is that time in a customer-vendor history when a customer first links with a new company for their information system provision. But, the desired loyalty arrangement comes in the later, on-going phase of the relationship.

By 1980, Burroughs Corporation was certainly a very established deliverer of computing products. One relatively new user, a community college in Michigan, had taken a contract with Burroughs for a B6800 installation prior to 1980 running it as a single-processor large system carrying both their academic and administrative programs.

A-NOTE

One of life's ironies in forcing career decisions produced an unexpected opportunity for me to become a Burroughs customer in 1980. MSC-Detroit, the central systems support organization, was in the process of experiencing newly mandated personnel shifts and creating some important relocation offers for personnel to consider. Each employee had to evaluate what type of work was being offered to them and where.

Very reluctantly, after reviewing the options, I elected to remain in the Michigan area and so found a position as a Director of Computer Services at a community college.

It was a very difficult decision for me. I enjoyed working for Burroughs but the available customer position involved a B6800 site and my heart and interests were with the large systems segment of the business and also with my life in Michigan.

A-NOTE

The retiring Director of Computer Services at the college was searching for a candidate to succeed him who understood the B6800 well and had some proven management experience. His own background had been with other computer manufacturers.

So, an opportunity opened for me to become a Burroughs customer. I would now be the one sitting at the head of the status meeting table and be the one responsible for running the show (hopefully).

The B6800/A5 Customer Site

The Michigan B6800 community college site had all its mainframe computing, both administrative and educational, on its one mainframe. The college was using various COBOL programs created in-house over the years, as most users were doing at the time. These unique programs needed local in-house support to maintain and update and faced the problems of having less than full documentation and resident knowledge of how they were created originally.

A community college site like this running both administrative and academic programs had the familiar customer requirements of:

- Guaranteed high uptime
- Capacity for heavy through-put loads at certain times

- Critical printing periods for grades and solid up-times during student registration periods
- Security concerns for a multi-use mainframe.
- Continuing load expansion needs
- Sufficient computer staffing to maintain the old programs and create new applications
- Maintain communication links between academic, administrative areas, and the computing team
- Maintain backup and recovery procedures
- Keep maintenance assurance and information flow with Burroughs, the vendor
- Implement the means to measure system performance for adjustments
- And, implement a User Request System to formally track user requests

Communications, Goals, Information Flow, Performance

Communications

Simple communications goals that surfaced to pursue were:

- Link with the local Burroughs sales and field engineering staff.
- Link with the community college staffs, educators, and students (the users)
- Link within the Computer Services group…inform and listen…team building

- Hold user status meetings with Burroughs present.

Information Flow to and from Burroughs

We in Computer Services insured information flow by:

- Requesting to attend CUBE with college representation
- Maintaining open lines of communication with the Burroughs Education
- Line-of Business group at Detroit World Headquarters
- \Providing for normal on-site sales and engineering discussion times.

Performance

We and our Operations Staff kept a strong eye on performance. (The staff never missed an end-of-semester grade printing run from 1980 through 1986):

- Problems were very few with the solid B6800 and later A5; they maintained very high up-time.
- The Systems DUMPANALYZER memory dump program and SPARK performance measuring software were used by our department, which were major tools to

deal with rapidly-changing system usage over the educational day.

- We kept up on product release levels to minimize missing any new fixes or features.

The B6800 was upgraded to an A5 in 1985 mainly for the "keeping-current" reason, with Burroughs recommendation.

Software Issues

A-NOTE

My Burroughs experience with large system user sites convinced me that using standardized software wherever possible was a direct help on controlling expensive programmer-analyst costs and helped avoid maintaining vast old software programs few people actually understood.

This site used SPARK and LINC II software packages, several popular languages for administrative use and teaching purposes, and supported a combination of in-house COBOL resident administrative and financial programs.

Burroughs Impact on the Site

166

The Burroughs Corporation

Burroughs Corporation in this time period (1980-1986) was a very mature company.

- This period was in the significant apex of Burroughs Corporation well-earned maturity in marketing hardware and software products.
- Hardware worked better than ever before in general in the mainframe field because of all the improvement in quality and performance done so intensely in the industry and by Burroughs.
- The time need needed for machine maintenance was spiraling down. Software attention for established products wasn't needed as often either as it had once been in earlier times.
- The Burroughs link with the site by Sales support and Field Engineering was comfortable and established.

Strengths of the Site

- Outstanding hardware and software performance
- Smooth transitions upward to an A5
- Smoothly working link to Burroughs support

Weaknesses of the Site

- Burroughs Education Line of Business

- There was a lack of available suitable standardized programs in the Burroughs higher education market to provide an easy bridging from a user's specific academic software needs to a workable, full-featured user program suite.
- Some large educational installations marketed their version of a universal higher-education programming set but generally the educational market sites were all still using some home-grown version set reflecting their specific needs.

What Was Happening Within Burroughs

- The concerns, planning and financial goals apparently going on within Burroughs under Blumenthal during the 1980-1986 period didn't have much impact on us at this site level. Those goals were mainly corporate issues and the only impact on a typical customer such as we were was for Burroughs to insure to continue providing new hardware and software options, which Burroughs did.
- The merger itself in 1986 didn't affect the site's daily running or its upgrade to an A5 but news of a merger of your vendor does become a topic for eventually evaluating down-the-road stability of a vendor and possible future supportability issues. We were aware of that.

A-NOTE

As a former Burroughs employee, I did remain having contact with some former employees, some of whom still worked at Burroughs when it merged in 1986. I knew the internal stories of how some Burroughs employees of all stations and levels dealt with the rapidly changing Burroughs of the early 1980's and its eventual merger. But, from a user's standpoint, the transition through a merger was Burroughs-professional and not an unmanageable upset.

End Result

- The B6800 and its successor A5 performed extremely well in the 1980 – 1986 period.
- As previously mentioned, there was a major need during the period for an up-to-date, available, suitably combined administrative and financial software system package that would fit the college's existing needs and be easily modified and maintained. Current user software systems marketed by some sites in the higher education field unfortunately weren't found suitable after a major search.
- The community college entered 1986 with Burroughs as its mainframe vendor on an A5 installation. Burroughs became Unisys. The college therefore became a Unisys site.

- The information systems challenges ahead then were focused on the long-range outlook for the mainframe support, the rapidly expanding PC curriculum challenges, and the looming requirement to tie all the information needs together on a suitable common system, integrating the smaller unattached computing satellite centers popping up in various administrative departments at the college.
- None of these goals were unusual in 1986. They defined most everybody in the educational business sector.

However, the B6800/A5 platforms have served faithfully and well up until this time and were a solid base for what was coming ahead for the college and Unisys.

A-NOTE

` **Personally, having the B6800/A5 platforms perform as they did while I was in a position of responsibility for the college information systems was in no small way a very supportive anchor to me and the job.**

Those Burroughs B6800/A5 mainframes had done the job and had done it well.

And, they were known quality products from a feisty, competitive company I knew something about.

Chapter 12

The Merger (1986)

The merger of the Burroughs Corporation and the Sperry Corporation became a reality in 1986. The merger was planned and completed by the Burroughs Corporation under the leadership of W. Michael Blumenthal who saw moving the Burroughs Corporation into a merger as the means to position the company to be a formidable No. 2 in the industry. Shortly after the merger, the new company was named The Unisys Corporation, a company still continuing to do business.

But, the significant Burroughs part of the story was in the lead-up to the merger in 1986.

Key Factors Driving the Merger

Burroughs was no stranger to acquisitions in its past. Acquisitions of both small and large enterprises to augment its needs were done and sprinkled all through-out the history of Burroughs, as outlined earlier in this book. But, the company had always run as the technically savvy, independent, far-back second major computer manufacturer and had stayed out of the early merging activities of their fellow competing companies who were disappearing through-out the 60's and 70's.

Mergers, on the other hand, are well-documented monumental undertakings in the business world and historically certainly not guaranteed to be producers of solutions for the original driving goals.

What was happening in the 1980's at Burroughs and in the computer industry, and in the American business world at large, were all brought to play in the proposed Burroughs – Sperry Merger.

The CEO

The merger surfaced under W. Michael Blumenthal's leadership. Like all CEO's in similar situations, he had the awesome job of weighing all the factors that went into the risk of a merger. His background and experiences played a major role in how he weighed those factors.

He was: an economist, an outsider to Burroughs, not a computer person, had been Secretary of Treasury for a time under President Carter, and had experience at Bendix Corporation in management. He was purposely chosen by Burroughs for these qualities he brought to the management job.

The Goal

The Burroughs Corporation

As W. Michael Blumenthal said himself, "No. 2 computer manufacturer was the goal".

John Markoff of the *New York Times* noted in 1990: "His (WMB) strategy was to create a fast-growing new force in the computer industry by capitalizing on trends that favored "open" standards of operating software, which make it easier for different manufacturers' computers to communicate."[140]

The *Palm Beach Post* printed a Reuters piece in 1986 noting: "WMB is maneuvering his newly created Unisys Corp, the world's second largest computer company, so that it will be one of the major players remaining in the year 2000."[141]

Also noting about Unisys, the article stated: "Computer industry analysts…cannot make a prognosis about Unisys' fate because of a lack of info about the company's long-term plans.

Unisys has more than a few challenges facing it in terms of:

> Integrating product lines
>
> Defining a long-term system of network strategy and developing future product lines"[142]

Blumenthal's Burroughs Environment

The Merger

1986 was a year of high activity, declining earnings and lean times, as the often changing computer industry market continued to boil.

In April, 1986, the *London Financial Times* reported: "As Burroughs' 66% first quarter earnings decline posted last week shows, it is a tough challenge..."[143]

Business Environment

The period of the 1980's was the dual presidency terms of Ronald Reagan.

Complicated and expensive corporate mergers were happening in the 1980's with mixed results. One goal for mergers appeared to be a hope for a more dynamic blending to emerge, with savings in duplication and new synergies for new products.

The book *Managing the Merger, Making it Work*, by Philip H. Mirvis and Mitchell Lee Marks, Prentice Hall, 1992, discusses the formation of Unisys from Burroughs and Sperry Corporations as one example of the complexities and hazards of attempting a merger.

In this book, the authors picked the Burroughs merger of 1986 as one of their featured merger stories to develop and analyze. That story provides a detailed analysis of what W, Michael Blumenthal and Burroughs wanted to accomplish in the merger and how the reality of the attempt played out soon after. The authors present the challenges and early results well.

Coincidentally, in 1983, the Bendix Corporation had merged to become the Allied Corporation. Bendix was, of course, Mr. Blumenthal's earlier corporate experience occurring before he went to the Carter Administration.

Early Rumblings

Early in Mr. Blumenthal's tenure at Burroughs, hints and forewarnings of an interest in mergers did surface in the media.

In 1981, the *New York Times* touched on the subject as well as looked at coincidental changes in ties between the Bendix Corporation (Mr. Blumenthal's former company in the Detroit area) and Burroughs that were of interest.

"Three directors resigned…(from) Bendix Corporation…to end intimate relationships with Burroughs?…all past or present members of the Burroughs Board. A 4th Bendix director on the Burroughs Board also resigned his seat. Why? Bendix may acquire someone? Burroughs? So, …no conflict, William M. Agee (of Bendix) said. Mr. Blumenthal had hired Mr. Agee while he ran Bendix.

Comment reported from Mr. Blumenthal, "Acquisitions? Total surprise to us."[144]

The Merger

From the *Detroit Free Press* April 5, 1984, "W. Michael Blumenthal said, "…no party had expressed an interest in acquiring or merging with Burroughs.""[145]

But, also in 1984, Burroughs was taking steps to protect itself in the world of mergers of the 1980's:

"Burroughs shareholders approved a plan today to make the Michigan computer company a less likely candidate for unwanted takeover attempts," W. Michael Blumenthal said.

The proposal…would increase the number of Burroughs common shares from 45 million to 120 million and create a new class of 40 million shares of preferred stock that the board could issue."[146]

In 1985, the *Wall Street Journal* picked up on the possible merger idea of Burroughs:

> "Burroughs and Sperry Corporation said they are discussing a merger. Computer industry analysts questioned the presumed strategy behind a Burroughs-Sperry merger. Burroughs' customer base: accounting and banking. Sperry: manufacturing, defense, and government."[147]

Merger Issues

There were major issues to be sure. The earlier cited book, *Managing the Merger*, goes over them well. It appeared to many of us on the sidelines who had worked for Burroughs that the company went for the merger decision in hopes of producing a new, even bigger and better company to run for a larger computer information system market position like IBM held. What Burroughs was doing worldwide at the time and the current competitive situation in the industry then had to play a very large part in helping Burroughs as a company assess the risk.

There were some very obvious merger and assimilation issues involved.

Both Burroughs and Sperry manufactured computer systems and neither product lines were compatible. Both companies had corporate structures understandably mostly in duplication because they were in the same business. Both companies had large customer bases with big investments at stake. In the high-cost business of purchasing or leasing computer systems, a buyer wanted assurances its vendor would be around for awhile. The topic of how long support could be expected played into these decisions as well. Careers at customers in the information industry depended on deciders making sound purchasing decisions and all that was in view when Burroughs became part of Unisys and its legendary company name was retired.

A-NOTE

The Burroughs name may have been retired in 1986 but remnants of the name continued showing up on such things as bank check book ledgers and other business forms.

B-NOTE

After the merger, the Unisys Corporation left Detroit and consolidated its main offices in Blue Bell, Pennsylvania. The Burroughs World Headquarters building is now home of the Ford Health System in Detroit.

Pros and Cons of the Merger

Pros

The *Wall Street Journal*, Europe Edition, printed specifics of the merger and Burroughs goals in mid-1985:

" Burroughs gave Sperry a deadline to accept the proposal today: 3.4 billion ($60 per share Sperry).

(Burroughs) started discussions about two months ago (April, '85) soon after Sperry's merger talks with ITT Corporation dissolved. (Burroughs) first bid unsuccessful.

Burroughs remains confident about its rationale for acquiring -

-   Significant cost savings in streamlining…efforts in procurement.
-   (Savings) in certain areas of research and development.
-   And in efforts in office-automation and communications products, a fast-growing segment; both companies are weak."[148]

Later, in 1986, Larry D. Duckworth, president, ICC of Cincinnati, had these thoughts:

-   IBM needs the pressure of a strong competitor to keep it sharp and innovative.
-   The user bases of both companies stand to gain from the merger.
-   Both Burroughs and Sperry have been putting a heavy commitment in to UNIX solutions.
-   …both companies have identified office automation as a key area and are already delivering products to meet emerging needs…"[149]

Cons

A trio of writers in the *Wall Street Journal* looked at the merger this way:

"…many analysts questioned the wisdom of such a merger. The combination would pair two companies heavily dependent on a dwindling share of the computer industry's most mature, slowest growing segment, mainframe computers.

And the combined company would still lack communications and desk-top computing techniques needed…

…other analysts said the possible attraction of a merger pale beside the technical problems of combining two companies with incompatible product lines selling to the same markets.

The writers also noted: …neither Sperry (who) acquired RCA in 1972 (or) Honeywell's takeover of GE's computer business did much against IBM."[150]

Several views of possible problems for the merger were expressed in the *London Financial Times* in an article titled: "Blueprint for a Digital Tower of Babel":

"The two companies are dissimilar in management style, marketing approach and product design. Burroughs has three incompatible architectures already in its product line and Sperry has four. (users ask to)...adopt a common interconnection standard. IBM SNA (System Network Architecture) links its systems. OSI (Open Systems Interconnection) plans for an international standard are advanced. Burroughs BNA (Burroughs Network Architecture)…(does have) gateways to communicate with OSI."

The article also looked at the rise of the PC market:

"…the whole market for the traditional mainframe is being upset by the advent of new companies offering "super-minis"-minicomputers using the most advanced electronics and are able to offer mainframe performance at minicomputer prices.

Also…(they use)…highly portable operating systems…such as UNIX, making it likely software...will in future, be simple to run on any machine."[151]

Blumenthal's Position

The merger was Mr. Blumenthal's decided goal. Early reports about the merger topic was out there already in 1985, if not earlier. The industry signs were eventually there. Mr. Blumenthal and the Burroughs Corporation were going for it.

It was accomplished in 1986.

The Merger Becomes Reality

"In June 1986, Burroughs agreed to acquire New York-based Sperry Corporation for $4.88 billion."[152]

And, one can imagine there was some relief at Burroughs when the news was also announced: "(Burroughs) profits increased 41% In the second quarter…(with) acceptance of the new A15 computer, despite attention of Sperry merger activity."[153]

The Merger

W.M. Blumenthal observed in October of 1986, "Combination with Sperry is proceeding smoother and faster than we had originally planned."[154]

Chapter 13

End-of-Job (EOJ)

Post-log (1968)

The 1968 merger of Burroughs with Sperry/Rand was the final major transition experienced by the historic Burroughs nameplate. The stated goal of that transition was to produce a new formidable information systems company from the merger that would combine resources, facilities, and strengths to rival the best in the business.

The results of that decision are now in the hands of history.

But, long before that decision, there were several earlier transitions that Burroughs faced that produced signature results which continually did pay off. Those transitions were why the Burroughs Corporation was in business for 101 years. Those earlier Burroughs transitions brought the company from a maker of modest mechanical adding machines to a builder of very large state-of-the-art computing mainframe systems.

The situation in 1986:

One of the major keys in the Burroughs business DNA that was present in 1968 was its ability to survive.

B-NOTE

Burroughs Key: (No. 20) Adapt, transform itself, and survive in business for 101 years

So, in 1968, the situation included factors such as:

1. The Unisys Corporation is created by a merger of Burroughs and Sperry/Rand (Unisys = **UN**ited **I**nformation **SYS**tems)
2. Burroughs and Sperry/Rand do continue in the information system business today as the historical basis of the merged company Unisys
3. Of the original Snow White and the Seven Dwarfs computer companies, all the other dwarfs are now gone from the business scene
4. The personal computer and versions of it are now a major global industry
5. Computing sites have mainly moved to decentralized networked nodes linked as systems
6. IBM remains a major presence in the information systems industry

The Burroughs Corporation

Major Contributions and Legacies of Burroughs (Summary)

The major contributions and legacies of Burroughs over the years are listed here as Burroughs Keys.

Burroughs Keys:

1. **Produce quality designs offering new features**
2. **Implement international marketing**
3. **Incorporate acquisitions into business plans**
4. **Market to defense business**
5. **Continually invest in Research and Development**
6. **Maximize crossover benefits from defense contracts**
7. **Normally promote from within for top management positions**
8. **Maintain core business while developing future products**
9. **Provide ease of use for customers**
10. **Identify and make best use of current and past assets**
11. **Employ diversity in employee hiring**
12. **Run lean with high employee responsibilities**
13. **Maintain two-way customer communication**
14. **Produce code-generating software**
15. **Utilize "Outsourcing" to supplement needs**
16. **Specialize in large scale and critical businesses**
17. **Provide total solutions for customers**
18. **Design for portability of products across machine lines**

19. Invest in training for both staff and customers
20. Adapt, transform itself, and survive in business for 101 years
21. Utilize a Line of Business (LOB) marketing focus

The Major Burroughs Transitions

From mechanical to electrical machines

From accounting machines to computers

From vacuum tubes designs to solid-state

From business machines to specialized defense designs

From small computers to large multi-processing machines

From basic designs to high-speed, secure, reliable systems

From standalone mainframes to large data communications linked systems

From mainframe focus only to evaluation of PC-like machines

From mainly financial business needs to full service computing across the industry

From standard software offerings to code-generating systems

Go to the outside world for their new CEO in 1979 rather than by usual in-house search

The Burroughs Corporation

And, the transition decision to merge Burroughs into a new entity, UNISYS

Looking Back

It would be very unfair to everyone concerned to try to second-guess decisions made by Burroughs management at the time decisions had to be made, especially in the light of now-past business and economic conditions at the time they were made. This book is a case study and personal chronicle of what happened, both good and bad. Therefore, all of it deserves consideration.

Emerging technologies, market movements, the factor of mergers viewed as popular for solutions to problems, and the entire force of world events were hurdles enough for anyone let alone a CEO trying to deal with them.

All those forces and more were entwined in each Burroughs transition decision.

Specific decisions that stand out now in retrospect were:

1. The pursuit of a strong main-fame business in a tightening market
2. The decision to not pursue a large-scale effort in mini-computer PC-style computers
3. The decision to broaden the company outlook and bring fresh ideas via a new CEO not an in-house computer man but one of economics, governmental, and local Bendix Corporation background

4. And, finally, the decision to merge with another
    similar computer company to produce a projected
    larger and stronger competing entity

Burroughs People in the Launch of Unisys

The initial management team announced for the new Unisys
Corporation of 1986 included many former Burroughs' names
and faces.

These remaining Burroughs managers and executives and the
legions of Burroughs employees who were still working for
Burroughs in 1986 became part of the core of the new company
and living keepers of the Burroughs past.

Some of the Burroughs notables at the launch included:

W. Michael Blumenthal, Chairman

Paul Stern, President

James A. Unruh, Executive Vice President

Fred R. Meier, VP for Corporate Program Management
and Office Product Operations

Michael A. Brewer, VP and Program General Manager,
Workstations and Office Systems

Arnold R. Newton, VP and Program General Manager of
Third Party/Cross Industry

The Burroughs Corporation

Jerry L. Peterson, VP and Program General Manager of Entry Level and Departmental Processors, UNIX-based Systems

Dagje Lacis, Education (Line of Business)

Plus, a long list of others in many diverse capacities who remained.

End-of-Job

The Burroughs Corporation

Chapter 14

Burroughs Basics

Overview

This chapter on Burroughs Basics is provided as a background reference discussion to show how the Burroughs Corporation was structured. For the non-Burroughs reader especially, this chapter describes the major parts of Burroughs, what was done where in the company, and by whom. Along with this road-map, there are explanations of what the many special names and terms used by Burroughs in their course of business meant.

As an example of a Burroughs customer point-of-contact, the Burroughs Corporation at its heights was a huge global enterprise but specifically, the Burroughs folks who may have serviced your local bank in New York, for instance, were members of a Burroughs Branch in the Business Machines Group that served all of North America. That branch relationship within a district and region and more is outlined in this chapter.

Basic Corporate Structure

All through its history, the Burroughs Corporation performed within a basic business structure that served it well. That basic business structure was changed and altered over the years but it remained the company core operating plan.

191

Burroughs, like most companies, changed as needed evaluating the evolving business organizational approaches that came along. The Burroughs era included that period when new ideas were coming out of Japan on how to structure business more effectively.

The general structure is described here noting that various modifications were made along the way to keep the company current.

The Burroughs base corporate structure was a familiar and popular sales-oriented structure of the time. It was a fairly straight-forward design similar to other corporations and computer companies. There was a Board, a Chairman, and a CEO; sometimes a President. The Board members reflected the style and makeup of most major companies by including business and community leaders of the day. The usual board member names were leaders in their fields but not necessarily in the computer field.

Within the Burroughs structure, Sales and Marketing people were the dominant players in the operational scheme. Authority flowed down through the Sales and Marketing structure. Sales called the shots.

In that structure, the Burroughs Corporate Offices were at the top and reporting to them were several key operating groups or divisions. Six representative operating groups (or divisions) Burroughs used are shown in Figure 1. Operating group titles changed over time but the six groups shown in the figure were typical Burroughs divisions.

The Burroughs Corporation

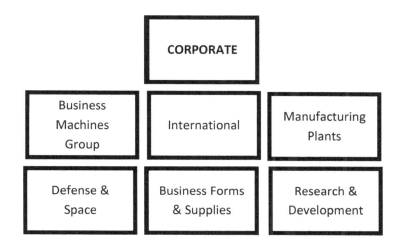

Figure 1

Basic Corporate Structure – Burroughs Corporation

The first group shown in Figure 1 is the Business Machines Group. It was the main North American computer marketing division. It was located in the Detroit World Headquarters. In fact, many of the Burroughs corporate offices were located in the World Headquarters Building in Detroit after 1970.

Figure 1 also shows five other representative operating groups Burroughs had:

- International
- Manufacturing Plants
- Defense & Space
- Business Forms & Supplies

- Research & Development

This list shows Burroughs was all along more than just a manufacturer of computers. Its total business offerings included the making of peripherals such as printers, tape drives, memory storage devices , and terminals. Burroughs built high-speed check and mail sorters. They continually produced business forms and supplies such as paper products, tapes and those check registers found in many checkbooks. And, they had a substantial defense industry group. This product diversification worked well for their continuing bottom line across the years.

Although Burroughs marketed in the USA through its Business Machines Group, it had a very substantial international marketing presence, too. That came out of its International Group . The broad reach of that group included Europe, United Kingdom, Mexico, Canada, South America and more.

Figure 1 then indicates the all-important manufacturing plants. Burroughs had plants in the United States and overseas as well. The many plants and locations were opened and closed as the business cycles and needs varied The Detroit area plants were part of the company's earlier history in that area and the later California plants followed the acquisition of ElectroData in Pasadena in 1957.

Following the plants in Figure 1 is the Defense and Space group located at Paoli, Pennsylvania.

In 1981, the Federal and Special Systems Group, which was a later Burroughs group, was active working on a 45.2 million Air Force contract.[155]

And, true to Burroughs style, there were significant Research \and Development facilities also but they were rarely publicized. Many of their locations were in specific plants

As mentioned previously, these groups were modified and changed as needed. In 1970, a split in the Business Machines Group created a new Systems and Manufacturing Group for development and manufacturing. The Business Machines Group remained the marketing arm.[156]

Business Machines Group (BMG)

The Business Machines Group (BMG) was the Burroughs group that covered the entire USA with a sales and marketing structure divided into Regions, Districts, and Branches. Each of these entities had a sales manager.

Supporting this sales structure were the Field Engineers (hardware) and the Systems Representatives (software) who worked on the machines at the customers' sites. The Field Engineers and the Systems Representatives had their own managers at Regional, District, and Branch levels to coordinate the technical support programs of the Business Machines Group.

In a sort of a dotted-line relationship, the technical people were in "staff" positions to the sales and marketing structure, which had the "line" employees or final deciders on business decisions.

The Regions

The functions of Sales and Marketing, Field Engineering, and Systems Support were laid out as previously mentioned in Regions, Districts, and Branches (See Figures 2 and 3).

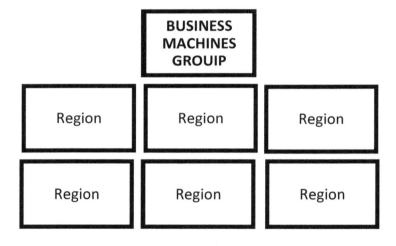

Figure 2

Regional Reporting Structure – Business Machines Group

The Regions (Figure 2) were designed to represent all of the major geographical portions of the USA market for the Business Machines Group. They were titled: "Southern", "Midwest", "Western", and so forth to denote their coverage areas. Regions were located in major US cities such as Detroit, Denver, Atlanta, etc.

The Burroughs Corporation

The Regions played a major role in the flow of business from BMG out to its eventual Districts and Branches. In a "centralized" approach to meeting customer needs, regional headquarters were often the location for highly specialized technical people and resources for specific service needs to their areas.

The Districts

The Districts existed within Regions and reported to them. They were important mainly as further responsive business links from the Regions to the Branches.

Districts were usually in large urban areas such as Chicago, Detroit, and so forth.

Districts, like Regions, often had specialized technical people who were available for temporary unique assignments as needed at their Branches.

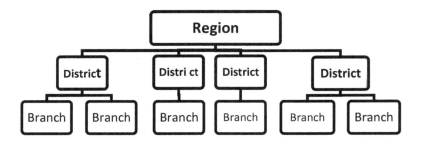

Figure 3

Regional District, and Branch Structure – Business Machines Group

The Branches

The branch was the Business Machines Group basic sales operating unit. From each branch customers were served for all their needs most directly.

The Branch was the Burroughs unit-office that each customer site was assigned.

The Branch service personnel Burroughs utilized for the customers included the Sales Representatives, Field Engineers, and System Representatives (See Figure 4).

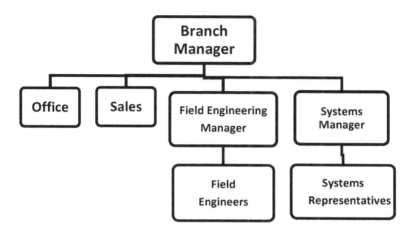

Figure 4

Branch Structure – Business Machines Group

Since Burroughs was structured similarly to other computer companies, the support personnel did functions similar with the others but often had slightly different job titles.

The machine support technicians were called "Field Engineers". The software support technicians were "Systems Representatives".

Branches could be generally inclusive of Burroughs products or could be specialized as "Financial" or "Commercial" if their

District was particularly broad. The Chicago District was such a District that had a Financial Branch.

Chapter 10 in this book is a chapter about life in the Burroughs Lansing, Michigan Branch, which was a very active multifunctional example of a full-service branch.

Line-Of-Business Marketing Structure (LOB) - Business Machines Group

At the corporate level, acting as a marketing focused umbrella, there was a group of marketing and planning groups organized along specific lines of business. These groups acted as coordinators of Burroughs products and thereby targeted user groupings which collectively would use similar specialized Burroughs products.

These groups were called "Line-Of-Business" Groups (LOB), and they included similarly oriented customer products such as those in: Education, Industry Marketing, Commercial, Manufacturing, Government, and Health as well as the Burroughs long-served Financial and Banking area, Another specific user group, the Defense and Space Group operated out of Paoli, Pa.

The Line-Of-Business (LOB) marketing grouping approach was designed to have designated groups working on specific marketing areas and able to coordinate product applications across those groupings.

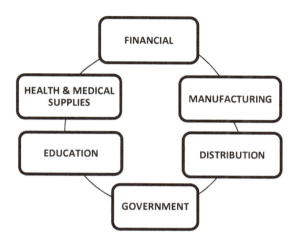

Figure 5

Line-Of-Business (LOB) Marketing Areas - Business Machines Group

Burroughs focused on several specific areas, with some modification of Line-of-Business general business grouping titles as needs dictated.

Major marketing areas served by the Line-Of-Business Groups included:

FINANCIAL

MANUFACTURING

DISTRIBUTION

GOVERNMENT

EDUCATION

HEALTH & MEDICAL FACILITIES

Burroughs used the Line-Of-Business concept of organizing marketing to focus on the company's key marketing areas to great advantage. Those areas represented key areas where Burroughs wanted to dominate: Financial, Manufacturing, Distribution, Government, Education, and Health & Medical facilities.

Each Line-Of-Business Group had an executive responsible for coordinating the group's marketing efforts and act as coordinator for the total LOB sales goals.

B-NOTE

Burroughs Key (No. 21) Utilize a Line-Of-Business (LOB) marketing focus

Field Marketing Manual (FMM)

The entire structure was operated under the Rules and Procedures of the Burroughs Field Marketing Manual (FMM) which was the guiding document constantly revised and updated to provide current operating procedures in effect through-out the organization.

The Field Marketing Manual (FMM) was the authorized guide for how the Burroughs Business Machines Group functioned. This document was the reference for all things corporate and was routinely modified and updated for its wide in-house user base.

Every Burroughs BMG worksite was directed by and bound by the FMM "word" for issues resolution.

Products

Software products made by Burroughs included operating systems, languages, specialized applications software, through-put and performance measuring programs, data-bases and data communications linking products, along with countless other products, including code-generating software in the later years. Code generating software allowed a user to create an entire software system far easier than designing original work in house with local analysts.

A partial list of Burroughs machine and software products is listed in Table A along with a representative listing of supporting manuals Burroughs published to support the products. The publishing dates of the manuals show a chronicled history of when the products entered the Burroughs marketing system.

Product Lines: Hardware and Software

Hardware

In its long history of doing business, everything from basic adding and accounting machines, typewriters, supplies and thence computers were marketed by Burroughs: The company also made letter sorting equipment and check processing machines as well as specialized military contracted products

Burroughs produced its familiar three series of computer machine lines from small to medium to very large through most of its later years.

But Burroughs was a wide-product manufacturing company. It marketed peripherals, business supplies and forms along with the computers and specialized machines.

During the Burroughs computer production years, technology used in the products ranged from vacuum tubes, and then First, Second, Third and Fourth generation solid-state products and then VSLI (Very Large Scale Integration).

Computer Hardware Product Naming Scheme

In 1967, Burroughs used a 3-digit numbering scheme preceded by a "B" to identify their early vacuum tube machines. Thus, the B205, B220, B340, etc.

The first large scale integrated circuit machine offered for sale by Burroughs used a 4-digit numbering scheme behind the letter "B". Thus, the B5500 (based on the B5000 System design).

The Burroughs Corporation

Using a "B" Prefix, a Machine Size Indicator, and a Design level, the naming scheme produced entries for the total Burroughs Small, Medium, and Large three-series scheme.

The first digit was the machine series identifier, the second digit indicated the version of the machine range. The third and fourth digits were model identifiers. Thus, there were B5000, B5500, B5700, and B5900 machines over the life of that particular "5000" size machine.

With that 4-digit scheme, Burroughs built and offered machines across the B1000/B2000/B3000/B4000/B5000/B6000/B7000/B8000 range supplying users with a choice of these models to fit into requirements for either a Small, Medium or Large System.

Two major changes to this numbering plan came in about 1980 when the Burroughs version of a PC came out as a B20 and B25 and in about 1983 when the final Burroughs large "A" series came out followed by the medium range "V" Series.

In Table A, representative Burroughs hardware and software technical support manuals are listed. They provide a good sample of computing products and the years in which they were introduced.

Software

Burroughs offered software products over four general areas:

Operating systems and operations management systems

Data-base, data communications systems, transaction-processing systems

Code generating software

Specific software for specific customer needs by industry requirements

Burroughs also offered software contracted programming services and outsource support.

Representative Software Products

Among its many software products, Burroughs offered:

Operating systems (MCP)

A-NOTE

MCP stood for Master Control Program. It was an operating system written in a form of the ALGOL programming language. That language allowed the operating system to be easily modified and expanded because of its design using "procedures' that could be coded independently and compiled back in for a new full-featured operating system quickly..

The Burroughs Corporation

The MCP was the useful technically advanced "heart" of the B5000 System when Burroughs introduced it.

- Languages: ALGOL, FORTRAN, BASIC, COBOL
- Specialized products: Data Communications, GEMCOS
- Data/Base, DMSII
- Problem-solving software: Memory Dump Analyzer
- Performance measuring software: SPARK
- Code-generating software: LINC II, GEMCOS

This is a partial list of some of Burroughs software products produced over time, particularly those marketed in the large systems range.

Key Plants and Operating Centers

To produce its variety of products, Burroughs had many plants in its domain over time. Sites at Pasadena, City of Industry, Mission Viejo, and Santa Barbara in were in California, There was a plant in Raritan in New Jersey, and a large systems defense-oriented plant in Paoli, Pa. Plus, there were additional plants at times elsewhere in the USA.

Burroughs Basics

Mentioned in this book were several of the Burroughs plants representative of the many plants and facilities built and closed over the Burroughs lifetime. (See Table C, Representative plants and facilities):

Tireman Rd, Plymouth plant, Wayne plant, Michigan

Santa Barbara, Pasadena, Mission Viejo, California (Also, City of Industry)

Paoli, Pennsylvania area facilities

Burroughs also had plants scattered overseas in the United Kingdom, Europe, and South America.

Supplies, peripherals and other business-oriented products were made at plants in Detroit such as the one at Tireman Road and the one in nearby Plymouth, Michigan. There were others in the USA doing the same work and also plants in international sites in the UK and Europe. Through-out its history, Burroughs had plants around the world producing peripherals and supplies for the "total user solution" plan.

Operating centers and offices mentioned in this book were:

World Headquarters, Detroit, Michigan

Central support Groups, Atlanta, Detroit, Paoli

The Burroughs Corporation

R & D Facilities (mainly in the plants; also Austin, TX)

Representative International plants included:

Seneffe, Belgium

Cumbernaud, Scotland

Strathleven, Scotland

Viers, France

In the Table A Internet References listing provided at the end of this book, one Website,

www.home.ix.netcom.com/~hancockm/manufacturing planys.htm,

maintained by Michael Hancock, includes an excellent reference table of Burroughs Manufacturing Plants by inception date and location.

The plant list changed and was modified often over the Burroughs history. Plants and centers came and went as needed. But the range of countries and USA locations shows the wide marketing and influence of Burroughs.

Acquisitions

Several important acquisitions by Burroughs have been mentioned throughout the book to show how important Burroughs regarded acquisitions as part of their business strategy.

The importance of acquisitions to Burroughs was it allowed them to add to their product offerings quickly by adding already viable companies like Memorex in the memory and tape area.

And, of course, the acquiring of ElectroData in 1957 was the significant critical move by Burroughs into the computing arena.

The website:

www.home.ix.netcom.com/~hancockm/mergers, etc.htm,

maintained by Michael Hancock, shows a more complete table of Burroughs Mergers, Acquisitions & Divestures by location and date.

Burroughs Customer Information Network

Product information was disseminated by and received into the corporation by several methods:

- Customer visits by Sales Representatives
- Burroughs Vendor-Customer User site status meetings

- CUBE (Cooperating users of Burroughs Equipment) semi-annual conferences
- Documentation on features, plans, specific topics, and how to use Burroughs products
- Technical release seminars and new product releases
- Training courses on-site and off-site at training locations (both employee and customer classes)
- On-site daily business flow between Burroughs technicians and customer staff

Burroughs Philosophies and Business Plans

Among Burroughs guiding principles that led to its long success were conscious efforts on:

- The Line-Of-Business concept to focus marketing and development energies
- The basic goal to provide the user greater ease of product use and versatility
- A continuing goal to increase machine speeds and capacities; to reduce component size
- A goal to insure high data security, reliability, restorability, large data capacity, and fast transaction rates

- Provide all the user's information and installation needs from one vendor source
- Keep the user's future viable and growing through major Research and   Development efforts
- Acquire what was needed to maintain being a full-service vendor
- Do global marketing across language and cultural boundaries
- Provide machine code for users to patch or modify at their sites if desired
- Utilize outsourcing to supplement technical needs when required (i.e. TATA of India)
- Provide formal training resources for both employees and customers

One final Burroughs basic feature stands out across its 101 years. Burroughs, though generally thought of as somewhat conservative in style, adapted, looked forward, listened to its customers, and persisted with its unwritten employee loyalty legacy to support it.

The Burroughs Corporation

Table A

Internet References

www.cbi.umn.edu/collections/inv/burros/

> Burroughs Corporation Records, Histories of Burroughs
> (CBI 90), Charles Babbage Institute, University of
> Minnesota, Minneapolis.

www.en.wikepedia.org/wiki/Burroughs_Corporation

www.en.wikipedia.org/wiki/Talk:Burroughs_Corporation

www.home.ix.netcom.com/~hancockm/history_timeline.htm

www.home.ix.netcom.com/~hancockm/merger_etc.htm

www.home.ix.netcom.com/~hancockm /burroughscorp.htm

www.home.ix.netcom.com/~hancockm/w_s_burroughs.htm

www.xnumber.com/xnumber/hancock7.htm

www.nytimes.com/1990/01/26/business/unisys-s-creator-stepping-down.html

www.unisys.com/about_unisys/history/index.htm

Table B

Representative Burroughs Reference Manuals

TITLE	SUBJECT	REF/NO.	DATE	NOTES
ALGOL	Programming	1019973	1964	Thurnau/Johnson/Ham
B5500 Handbook	Disk/Data Comm	0131986	10/67	MCP
B6500/B7500	Stack Mechanism	1035441	1968	Hauck & Dent
B340	Reference Manual\	1037215	6/68	Operating Instructions
B5500/ALGOL	Extended Reference	1028024	7/68	
B5500 Time Sharing	Terminal User's	1038205	8/68	Guide
B5500 FORTRAN	Compiler Reference	1032083	9/68	
BIPS-1	Integer	1040136	1/69	Programming
B300/500/5500	Audio Response	1040474	2/69	System
B6500	Process Handling	1051281	8/69	J. C. Cleary
Basic I/O Handling	B6500	1051752	10/69	Rajini M Patel
B6500 ALGOL	Extended Reference	1039559	1/70	Manual

The Burroughs Corporation

TITLE		SUBJECT	REF/NO.
	DATE	NOTES	
B6500 MCP		Reference Manual	1042447
	2/70		
B6500		Data Comm	1045648
	2/70	Functional Description	
6500 Data Comm		Processor Reference	1044831
	2/70		
B6500 Hot Line		B6500	1042298-004
		Questions & Answers	
B2500/B3500 PCS		Production Control	1044930
	4/70	System Reference Manual	
FORTRAN		Self-Learner	1045697
	7/70		
B6700 MCP		Informational	5000086
	11/70	Manual	
B6700		Dump/Analyzer	5000334
	5/71	System	
Data Communicator		Introduction to	1059086-026
		Data Comm	
	1971	B300/500/2500/3500/	
		4500/5700/6700/DC100	
INFOSYS		Programming Techniques	N/A
	4/72	ALGOL	
B6700/B7700		CANDE Command	5000381
		& Edit Language	
	10/72	Info Manual	

TITLE	SUBJECT	REF/NO.
DATE	NOTES	

B6700 Handbook	Vol. 1 Hardware	5000276
1/72		
B6700	Reference	1058633
5/72		
Medium Systems	Reference Manual	1063773
12/72 I-O & Data Comm		
B6700/B7700	System Software	5000722
7/73 Handbook		
B7700 Systems	Characteristics	1059979
1/73 Manual		
B6800	Systems Concepts	N/A
N/A Binder		
Creative Solutions	In Industry – Ford	1073988
4/74		
Data Management	B6700/B7700	5000235
1/73		
DMSII DASDL	Reference	5001084
10/75 Mark II.7 Release		
DMSII Host Language		5000839
4/74 Reference		
B6700 SPARK	Sampler; Analyzer	5000920
6/75 MK 2.5,6,7 Release		
B6700 SPARK	Codeanalyzer	5000938
6/75 MK 2.5,6,7 Release		
B6700 SPARK	Logstatistics	5000946
6/75 MK 2.5,6,7 Release		
Lectures	Structured	2011656
12/76 Programming Techniques		

TITLE		SUBJECT	REF/NO.
DATE	NOTES		
Lectures		TEMPO Math	2011532
3/77	Program Optimization		
Lectures		BASIS Statistical	2010070
3/77	System Techniques		
B6700/B7700		ALGOL Reference	5000649
5/74	Mark II.5 Release		
B7700/B6000		GEMCOS Message	1096567
11/76	Control User's Reference		
B7700/B6000		GEMCOS	1100211
2/77	Capabilities		
B7000/B6000 RJE		Remote Job Entry	5001548
4/77	Reference Manual		
B7000/B6000		BINDER	5001456
5/77	Reference Manual		
B7000/B6000 WFL		Work Flow	5001555
6/77	Language Reference Manual		
B7000/B6000		Diagnostic MCS	5001514
6/77	Reference Manual		
B7000/B6000		NDL Reference	5001522
9/77	Manual		
B7000/B6000		ALGOL Reference	5001639
5/77	Manual		
B7000/B6000		DMSII Inquiry	5001472
9/77	Reference		
B7000/B6000		DMSAII DASDL	5001480
3/78	Reference		
Dictionary		X3 Technical	1108677
		Report- American National	
9/77	Standard		

TITLE	SUBJECT	REF/NO.
	DATE NOTES	
B6800 Global	Operation &	5010218
2/79	Maintenance Global	
	Memory Volume 1	
LINC II	Language	1198223
8/86	Reference Software Generator	
LINC II	Student Guide	N/A
12/86	Software Generator	
Demo (900 series)	Large Systems	N/A
11/81	MSC-Central, MK3.2	

The Burroughs Corporation

Table C

Representative Burroughs Plants and Facilities

USA

Carlsbad	California
Coral Sp[rings	Florida
Hollywood	Florida
Jacksonville	Florida
Piscataway	New Jersey
Plainfield	New Jersey
Raritan	New Jersey
Lisle	Illinois
Paoli	Pennsylvania
Mission Viejo	California
Westlake	California
Plymouth	Michigan
Tireman	Michigan
Wayne	Pennsylvania
Tredyffrin	Pennsylvania
Thousand Oaks	California
Rancho Bernardo	California
Santa Barbara	California
City of Industry	California
Pasadena	California
World Headquarters	Michigan

INTERNATIONAL

Liege	Belgium
Seneffe	Belgium
Sao Paolo	Brazil
Nottingham	England
Pantin	France
Viller-Escalles	France
Cumbernaud	Scotland
Edinburgh	Scotland
Glenrothes	Scotland
Strathleven	Scotland
Lima	Peru
Quadalarja	Mexico

Notes

Chapter 1

1. "UNISYS, About Unisys, Unisys – A History of Excellence",
   www.unisys.com/about_unisys/history/index.htm
2. "Who's Who?", W.S. Burroughs,
   www.home.ix.netcom.com/~hancockm/w_s_burroughs.
   htm
3 Michael Hancock, "Burroughs Adding Machine
   Company, Glimpses Into the Past,   History – *1857-1953*",
   www.xnumber.com/xnumber/hancock7.htm
4. Ibid.
5. Ibid.
6. Ibid.
7. Ibid.
8. Ibid.
9. Ibid.
10. Michael Hancock, "Historical Timeline of the Burroughs
    Adding Machine Company (1857-1962)",
    www.home.ix.netcom.com/~hancockm/history_timeline.
    htm

Chapter 2

11. "Burroughs, Growth & Profits Through Research & New Ideas", Paine Webber, Jackson, Curtis, 1961

12. Computer History Museum –" Timeline of Computer History", www.computerhistory.org

13. Ibid.

14. www.home.icx.netcom.com/~hancockm/history_timeline.htm

15. www.en.wikipedia.org/wiki/Burroughs_Corporation

16. www.home.icx.netcom.com/~hancockm/history_timeline.htm

17. www.home.ix.netcom.com/~hancockm/history_timeline.htm

18. Ibid.

19. Ibid.

20. "Burroughs, Growth & Profits Through Research and New Ideas", Paine, Webber, Jackson, Curtis, 1961

21. **www.home.ix.netcom.com/~hancockm/history_timeline.** htm

22. Ibid.

23. www.home.ix.netcom.com/~hancockm/mergers,_etc.htm

24. Ibid.

Chapter 3

25. *BEMA News Bulletin*, February 7, 1966

26. *New York Times,* February 17, 1961

27. *New York Times*, September 20, 1961

28. *Electronic* News, August 12, 1963

29. Ibid.

30. *Detroit News*, Jack Crellin, January 14, 1964

31. Ibid.

32. *BEMA News Bulletin*, May 16, 1966
33. *EDP Weekly*, July 14, 1966
34. *EDP Weekly,* September 12, 1966
35. Jim Collins, *Good to Great*
36. *Unisys History Newsletter*, Vol.3, No.1, "Some Burroughs Transistor Computers" by George Gray.
37. *BEMA News Bulletin*, November 28, 1966
38. *Detroit News*, Pictorial Sunday, February 1, 1959
39. *Modern Data*, April, 1972
40. *FORBES*, "Anatomy of a Turnaround", November 1, 1968
41. Ray W. Macdonald, "The Transition of Burroughs," 1975 Business Leadership Award, UM Grad School of Business Administration
42. Burroughs B 5000 Conference, OH 98, Oral history on 6 September 1985, Marina del Ray, California. Charles Babbage Institute, University of Minnesota, Minneapolis.
43. *BEMA News*, June 24, 1963
44. *Wall Street Journal*, November 1966
45. Ibid.

Chapter 4

46. *Wall Street Journal*, "Ray Macdonald is CEO", February 1, 1966
47. *Detroit News,* April 14, 1970
48. *EDP Daily*, July 15, 1970
49. *Wall Street Journal*, EDP Industry Report, May 14, 1970
50. The *Detroit Free Press*, October 10, 1970

51. *Wall Street Journal,* October 7, 1970

52. *BEMA News Bulletin,* February 7, 1966

53. *BEMA News Bulletin*, N.Y., November 18, 1968

54. *Michigan Contractor-Builder*, April 15, 1972

55. *New Center News*, June 26, 1967

56. *Detroit Free Press*, June 10, 1984

57. *Detroit News*, "Burroughs: A Super Salesman Pushes The Buttons", John J. Green, November 11, 1970

58. Ibid.

59. *Business Week*, March 11, 1967

60. *Wall Street Journal*, Scott R Schmedal, October 7, 1970

61. *Wall Street Journal*, March 25, 1970

62. *Information Week*, February 23, 1970

63. *New Center News*, Detroit, December 3, 1973

64. *COMPUTERWORLD*, December 17, 1975

65. *Wall Street Journal*, August 3, 1979

66. *Buffalo Evening News*, Trammel, Knights-Kent, Saxx, January, 2, 1981

66. *Wall Street Journal*, Dallas, TX, January 16, 1969

68. *Communications News*, Wheaton, IL, May, 1969

69. *Chicago American Today*, August 4, 1969

70. The *Kansas City Star*, October 23, 1970

71. *Wall Street Journal*, Dan Dorfman, November 3, 1972

72. *COMPUTERWORLD*, Michael Merritt, March 17, 1971

73. *FORBES*, "Burroughs Corporation: Sophisticated Buggy Whips", February 15, 1966

74. *University of Michigan Business Review*, 1975, "The Transition of Burroughs", Ray W.

Macdonald

Chapter 5

75. *Call*, Piqua, Ohio, November 20, 1980

Chapter 6

Chapter 7

76. *Business Week,* "The Burroughs Syndrome",
November 12, 1979
77. *Business Week*, "The Burroughs Syndrome",
March 12, 1979
78. *Business Week*, "The Burroughs Syndrome",
November 12, 1979

Chapter 8

79. *DATAMATION*, June 1969.

Chapter 9

80. *Florida Times Unio*n", by Edwin McDowell, N. Y. Times
News Service, November 30, 1980
81. *Electronic News*, October 22, 1979
82. *Business Week,* November 12, 1979
83. *NEWSWEEK*, October 29, 1979
84. Ibid.
85. *Business Week*, "Executive Suite", October 29, 1979

86. *Business Journal*, November 12, 1979

87. *Wall Street Journal*, April 21, 1981

88. Edwin McDowell, *Florida Times Union*, N.Y. Times News Service, November 30, 1980

89. *Detroit Free Press*, November 4, 1980

90. "Ticker Talk", Morris Levine, February 15, 1981

91. *Buckeye Business Journal*, December 11, 1980

92. *Syracuse Herald Journal* ,N.Y. December 15, 1980

93. Ibid, "More on WMB"

94. Mike Scanlon, *Farmington Observer*, March 19, 1981

95. *The Miami Herald*, April, 22, 1981

96. Monte I. Trammel, The *Detroit Free Press*, April 21, 1981

97. Jerrold S. Foley, Burroughs Corp., *Data Communications*, February 1983

98. *Suburban & Wayne Times*, Wayne, PA, October 30, 1980

99. *News Press*, Chattanooga, T, July 16, 1980

100. *Suburban Register*, Malvern, PA, February 12, 1981

101. *Business Week*, November 12, 1979

102. *Detroit Free Press*, Monte I. Trammel, April 21 1981

103. *Focus*, Philadelphia, "The changing computer industry", April 8, 1981

104. *Detroit Free Press*, Ted Withington, analyst, Arthur D. Little, January 24, 1984

105. *FORBES*, N.Y. "Room at the Top", Barry Stavro, November 14, 1985

106. *Detroit Free Press*, February 19, 1984

107. *Detroit Free Press*, September 23, 1980

108. The *Detroit News*, David McNaughton, , February 1984

109. *Progress Bulletin*, Pomona, California, June 20, 1980

110. *Clearwater Sun*, Florida, November August 1980

111. *Sun*, Georgetown, Texas, February 8, 1981
112. *Ft. Lauderdale News*, February 10, 1981
113. C. I. Babbage Institute, University of
      Minnesota, Press Clippings, Burroughs,
      Box CB190
114. Ibid.
115. Ibid.
116. *Journal of Commerce*, N.Y.,
      March 16, 1981
117. *1ˢᵗ Quarter Review*, Burroughs Corp., 1985
118. *L.A. Times,* "Business", February 17, 1980
119. *Electronic News*, N.Y., November 17, 1980
120. *DATAMATION*, N.Y., November 1980
121. *DATAMATION*, N.Y., April 1981
122. *Word/Processing World*, N.Y., June 1980
123. *Information System News*, Manhasset, N.Y.,
      April 6, 1981
124. The *Wall Street Journal*, March 27, 1985
125. Ibid.
126 . *Ist Quarter Review*, Burroughs Corp, 1984
127. *Government Computer News*, Silver Spring,
      Maryland, December 6, 1985
128. *COMPUTERWORLD*, April 1, 1985
129. *COMPUTERWORLD*, November 11, 1985
130. Jerrold S. Foley, Burroughs, Corp., *Data
      Communications*, February 1983
131. *Farmington Observer*, Mike Scanlon, March
      19, 1981

132. Judy Harrison, Asst. Ed, "Silent Burroughs changes image; makes a lot of Noise", *Computer & Electronics Marketing*, 1984

133. *Business Week*, November 12, 1979

134. Judy Harrison, Asst. Ed, "Silent Burroughs changes image; makes a lot of Noise", *Computer & Electronics Marketing*, 1984.

135. *Burroughs First Quarter Highlights 1984*, "Burroughs looks like a Contender again", January 24, 1984

136. *DATALINK*, Adam Page, May 6, 1985

137. Russell Mitchell, Gordon Bock, "Can Burroughs Break Out of the BUNCH in the Mainframe Race?", *Business Week*, December 9, 1985

138. *Electronic News*, N.Y. November 24, 1980

Chapter 10 MSC

139. *Electronic News Weekly*, February 2, 1981

Chapter 11 User

Chapter 12 Merger

140. John Markoff, The *New York Times*, "Unisys Creator Stepping Down", January 26, 1990

141.   Jane Light, "UNISYS Sets Goal For 2000", Reuters, *Palm Beach Post*, November 22, 1986

142.   Ibid.
143.   *The London Financial Times*, Paul Taylor, in N.Y., April 23, 1986
144.   *New York. Times*, February 28, 1981
145.   "Burroughs 2nd Quarter Review ", 1984
146.   The *Washington Post*, April 5, 1984
147.   The *Wall Street Journal*, June 14, 1985
148.   The *Wall Street Journal, Europe Edition*, Dale D. Buss, June 17, 1985
149.   *Information Week*, "Let's admit what's good about the Burroughs-Sperry Merger", Larry D. Duckworth, June 23, 1986
150.   The *Wall Street Journal,*. John Marcom, Jr., James B. Stewart, Dale B. Buss, June 14, 1985
151.   *London Financial Times,* "Blueprint for a Digital Tower of Babel", May 30, 1986
152.   The *Detroit News,* July 17, 1986
153.   Ibid.
154.   The *Denver Post,* October 17, 1986

Chapter 13 EOJ

Chapter 14 Basics

155. *Surcrean Register*, Malvern,PA, February 12, 1982.

156. *Detroit Free Press*, June 20, 1970

www.ingramcontent.com/pod-product-compliance
Lightning Source LLC
Chambersburg PA
CBHW051229050326
40689CB00007B/850